Kuth / Ranieri Architects

Graham Foundation / Princeton Architectural Press series

New Voices in Architecture
presents first monographs on emerging designers from around the world

An Architecture of the Ozarks: The Works of Marlon Blackwell

ARO: Architecture Research Office

Charles Rose, Architect

Julie Snow Architects

Leven Betts: Pattern Recognition

Lewis.Tsurumaki.Lewis: Opportunistic Architecture

Plain Modern: The Architecture of Brian MacKay-Lyons

Rick Joy: Desert Works

Think/Make: Della Valle Bernheimer

VJAA: Vincent James Associates Architects

Kuth/Ranieri Architects

Byron Kuth and Elizabeth Ranieri

With texts by Ila Berman, Mitchell Schwarzer, Rodolphe el-Khoury, and Aaron Betsky

Graham Foundation for Advanced Studies in the Fine Arts, Chicago
Princeton Architectural Press, New York

For Addi, Franny, and Grace

Princeton Architectural Press/Graham Foundation
New Voices in Architecture

Published by
Princeton Architectural Press
37 East Seventh Street
New York, New York 10003

For a free catalog of books, call 1.800.722.6657.
Visit our website at www.papress.com.

All images courtesy Kuth/Ranieri Architects unless otherwise noted.
ii, 6L, 7, 9, 11C, 12, 13, 15, 17, 19, 20T, 21B, 22T, 23, 24, 33B: Cesar Rubio
5, 10: © David Wakely
6TR: Florence Lipsky, *San Francisco: La grille sur les collines* (Marseilles: Editions
    Parenthèses, 1999), 151.
8T, 8C, 14T, 69, 70L, 71L, 72, 73C, 74–76, 77T, 78C, 79: Jeremy Jachym
14C: Sally Schoolmaster
18L, 27, 28, 29C, 30T, 30C, 31, 32T, 34, 35, 37, 38, 39C, 40T, 41–43, 44T, 44C, 45, 55, 56,
    57B, 58C, 59, 60, 61T, 61C, 62C, 63, 64C, 65, 66T, 67B, 173 fig. 10: Sharon Risedorph
47, 48T, 49, 50T, 51–53, 83C, 87BR, 88–89: Joe Fletcher
56L: Ron Lutsko, Jr.
81T, 82, 84T, 85B, 86TL, 86B, 87T, 87BL, 90T, 91C, 103C: Felipe Villas Boas
92, 117: courtesy SFMOMA
161T, bird images, left to right: Tom Merigan, Tom Merigan, Greg Lavaty, Jeff Poklen,
    Glen Tepke

Every reasonable attempt has been made to identify owners of copyright.
Errors or omissions will be corrected in subsequent editions.

Project Editor: Clare Jacobson
Copy Editor: Mark Woodworth
Designer: Jan Haux

Special thanks to: Nettie Aljian, Bree Anne Apperley, Sara Bader, Nicola Bednarek,
Janet Behning, Becca Casbon, Carina Cha, Penny (Yuen Pik) Chu, Carolyn Deuschle,
Russell Fernandez, Pete Fitzpatrick, Wendy Fuller, Erin Kim, Aileen Kwun, Nancy
Eklund Later, Linda Lee, Laurie Manfra, John Myers, Katharine Myers, Daniel Simon,
Andrew Stepanian, Katie Stokien, Jennifer Thompson, Paul Wagner, Joseph Weston,
and Deb Wood of Princeton Architectural Press —Kevin C. Lippert, publisher

Library of Congress Cataloging-in-Publication Data
Kuth, Byron (Byron Dean), 1953–
Kuth/Ranieri Architects / Byron Kuth and Elizabeth Ranieri ; with texts by
Ila Berman ... [et al.].
  p. cm.
Includes bibliographical references and index.
ISBN 978-1-56898-865-8 (alk. paper)
1. Kuth/Ranieri Architects. 2. Architecture—United States—History—20th
century. 3. Architecture—United States—History—21st century. I. Ranieri,
Elizabeth (Elizabeth Sarsfield), 1963– II. Berman, Ila (Ila Leslie), 1960– III. Title.
NA737.K88K88 2010
720.092'2—dc22
                                                        2009016252

Contents

Preface

We arrived in the Bay Area just prior to the Loma Prieta earthquake and established Kuth/Ranieri Architects in 1990. The studio began in a San Francisco industrial space South of Market during the rise of the dotcom era. Against the background of this dynamic and unpredictable locale and economy, our work has been largely influenced by the region's uniqueness, its progressive culture, exceptional beauty, and landscape. Having split our time over the last two decades between teaching, building, and research, we've produced a broad spectrum of projects, from small-scaled objects, installations, and buildings that explore tactile and visceral experiences of environments to architectural and urban design proposals that investigate more universal problems of building, culture, and global environments.

      The compilation of the materials within this book has given us the opportunity to present ideas within our work that navigate a cultural territory of sustainability and continue to inform our practice and the discipline at large. Central to all of the projects is an amplification of craft in the artifact. Our intention is to arrive at an open-ended proposition that favors a performative approach over a formal one. The preoccupation and deployment of materials, components, and systems signal our effort to precisely measure things that are often indeterminate or unknown: the latent aspects inherent in each investigation, site, or program. As our practice matures, the work evolves toward a consistent position in which sustainable strategies push beyond building performance to focus on developing an expressive environmental architecture.

Byron Kuth
Elizabeth Ranieri

Acknowledgments

We wish to acknowledge the following:

Our families and parents, Marion Greene, James Kuth, and Donald and Mary Elizabeth Ranieri, both for introducing us to the pleasure of buildings and drawing at an early age, and for their ongoing support throughout our careers. Steve Const, our associate partner, friend, and much more. A deep and always renewing appreciation to those who shaped our education, showing us light where there was already light: Eve Blau, Michael Hays, Jeffery Katz, Rodolfo Machado, George Wagner, and Judith Wolin. A more significant part of our education, of course, are our dear friends and colleagues Nader Tehrani, a longtime friend and soul mate, and Rodolphe el-Khoury, collaborator and sage. To Bill Stout and Paulett Taggart, with affection and unending respect. To Aaron Betsky, who believed in us and made sure we always hewed to the wild side; Ila Berman, who graciously agreed to write for us and is a great advocate of thoughtful design. Over the years, so many people have changed how we think, make, and feel, by their insights and support: Fariborz Amini, David Brisson, Craig Hartman, Ann Hatch, Adriane Iaan and Christian Stolz, James Martin, David Meckel, Margaret Ranieri, Ann Rieselbach, Adi Shamir, Sarah Herda, and Mark Simon. And to the two people who made this book possible, Gretta Tritch and our editor, Clare Jacobson. We thank you all.

Introduction: Paradoxical Matters

Ila Berman

The construction of a monograph on one's own work is, in itself, both a design project and a critical act. It is at once the making of something, not unlike the making of a work of architecture, and the consolidation and analysis of an exploratory body of research that is initially somewhat geological in character—composed of thick layers of strata, each of which has a degree of consistency defined by the materials and forces that shaped its development. For Byron Kuth and Elizabeth Ranieri, the making of this book thus entails cutting into this thickened terrain, with the explicit purpose of exposing a cross section of their practice that might otherwise have remained embedded—hidden behind the contextual circumstances and material specificity of each project's evolution. The cross section that they unearth, and then carefully reassemble, shows both the operative consistency and the variability of their practice, one that extends from the intimacy of microscaled handheld artifacts to the expansiveness of macroscaled infrastructural landscapes, and that ranges in focus, temperament, and technique as one moves from their skillfully designed residential built works (comprising the first section of this book) to their more experimental research endeavors and highly provocative installations. In this process, Kuth and Ranieri draw on the historian's comprehension of context, the theorist's inventory of concepts, and the critic's tools of interrogation, through which the documentation of their firm's genesis might be positioned, thought, and unfolded. Three external voices—of Mitchell Schwarzer, Rodolphe el-Khoury, and Aaron Betsky—that are inserted at the center of this volume, begin to resonate differently with the many complex facets of the works presented while elaborating an expanded disciplinary network within which Kuth/Ranieri's architectural practice might be situated. Additionally, these texts promote the validation of the firm's performative milieu and contribute to the creative construction of its evolving identity.

The compilation of such a book is therefore neither a simple act nor a singular one. It is an undertaking that allows for selective introspection while enabling a mode of reframing that might be said to both precede and follow the making of the identity of a practice. In the case of Kuth/Ranieri, the question of identity is a difficult one—perhaps because, by implication, we assume identities to be characteristically singular, consistent, and recognizable. Such identities, however, are precisely those that constitute the impossible terrain that Kuth/Ranieri's projects have always sought to investigate—those spatial, material, and symbolic "truths" handed down to us from our modern predecessors that have become the extended subjects of inquiry in each of the works presented in this monograph. If there can be said to be one critical trajectory that traverses the scalar and typological range of works presented, it is the unraveling or blocking of identity that is somehow consistently repeated throughout this work, each time encountered through buildings, installations, and research projects that make manifest the hidden paradoxes and latent complexities embodied within the singular architectural act. This is work that refuses the easily apprehensible and denaturalizes the very context of its own making, asking us to question the possibility of architecture's simple legibility, its "transparency," even within the familiar realms of the domestic and the everyday, or the reality-driven domains of the civic, the infrastructural, and the technological.

Within Kuth/Ranieri's built residential projects, reality is initially conferred by the fact of each building's constructed physicality. Yet each exquisitely crafted detail implanted within these works becomes a commentary on the making of this reality as well as on its own characterization as a singular and individuated object—its multiplicity of meanings and dense materiality intent on exploding the boundaries of the actual space it so carefully defines. These works make explicit the "return of the repressed," as both sense and sensation are reinserted into the abstract spatiality of an expanded modernist practice, disturbing the dimensional clarity on which such spaces traditionally depend. Here, the complex valuation of meaning and experience becomes immediately evident, whereby the technological expression of the detail, for example, adeptly reappropriated for nonutilitarian purposes, allows for a critical reinterpretation of the sublimation of function in the wake (or perhaps now only faint reverberations) of modernism's instrumentalization of space and matter. The consistent richness and precision of this firm's work, an enormous accomplishment in its own right, thus becomes a veil to another, less easily classifiable project, where meaning and making bifurcate and intertwine, germinating the seeds of a complex embodied intelligence found at the very roots of this experimental architectural practice. The idea of a subject (or practice) split between the worlds of thought and matter, provisionally given to us in the two parts of this book—the first dedicated to built projects and the second to speculative research projects—is therefore perhaps another legible taxonomy whose identity is already undone from within, overturned by the intricate interweaving of research and practice that underscores all the works that fill this volume.

Although certainly consistent, the larger trajectory of Kuth/Ranieri is also variable and evolutionary in character. Unlike practices whose identities are based on fixed typologies recognizable through the repetition of a figure or a set of organizational characteristics—a stylistic signature—Kuth/Ranieri's practice is highly operative in nature. Theirs is a practice whose mode of repetition is tied to concepts and strategies, rather than to a collection of discernible forms, and this enables evolution through the application of the former to an expanded field of changing contexts and research agendas. Thus, despite the more obvious differences in scale, content, and materiality between the projects represented in the two halves of this book, their relationship resides in the more subtle conceptual approaches and tactical procedures that bind these two halves together. The network of complex details so evident in the earlier residences, for example, finds its repetition in proposed projects such as Mission Bay, whose field is defined by carefully placed ecological insertions—urban details (both natural and artificial, wild and domesticated)—that, not unlike those details embedded within their built projects, are characterized by paradox and saturated with material intensity. These synthetic yet highly charged moments, interruptions that ask us to question the ease with which we recognize the world around us, are perhaps the most significant markers of these architects' evolving critical practice. Throughout all the works presented herein, Byron Kuth and Elizabeth Ranieri consistently challenge the simple identity of architecture. They create carefully designed architectural artifacts and urban landscapes that, by amplifying our perceptual intelligence, disrupt the factual and the familiar, and reveal to us another world that is hidden below, behind, or beyond the one we already claim to know.

Nob Hill Residence

San Francisco

The house is sited on a narrow alley that transforms from street to garden at the building's front door. The project falls between the city grid and the organic nature of the San Francisco landscape. Vistas from the house include Pacific Heights, the Golden Gate Bridge, and the distant hills of Marin County to the north. The planning of each floor remains open to the views, with the central living spaces bracketed by perimeter cores. Wall surfaces are expressed as cabinetry, concealing and containing stairs, storage, and baths; surfaces unfold, slide, and disappear, actively signifying and responding to the programs they serve.

Like the plan, the facade responds to the site and context with the transformation of typical, typological elements specific to urban residences in San Francisco. The bay window, entry, front-facing garage door, and street-side roof terrace are folded into a singular assembly of clear sealed mahogany panels and ledges. The regimented order of the horizontal ledges is set in contrast to the inflection and modulation of the facade's planar surfaces. The facade's interplay of regular and indeterminate geometry relates the Cartesian orders of the city to the exaggerated topography of its landform.

SKIN/surface: The finely articulated skin transforms the dimensionality of the neutral planes of modernism into the directionality of the continuous folded surface. This woven surface oscillates between frame and fill, its rhythmic seriality acting to simultaneously synthesize and expose difference. The compression and expansion of horizontal striations that trace this skin, and the subtle local inflections of its surface, imbue space with a corporeal thickness that converts the faciality of the facade into a new material body.
–I. B.

Sections, railing detail

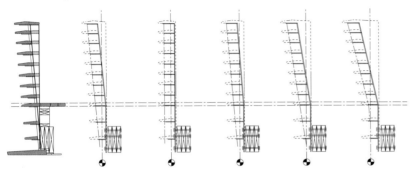

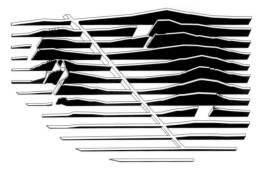

Axonometric, parallel streets in San Francisco

Site plan

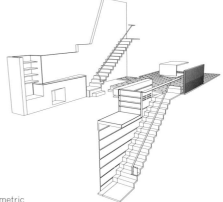

Circulation axonometric

Plan, first level

1. Kitchen
2. Dining
3. Living room

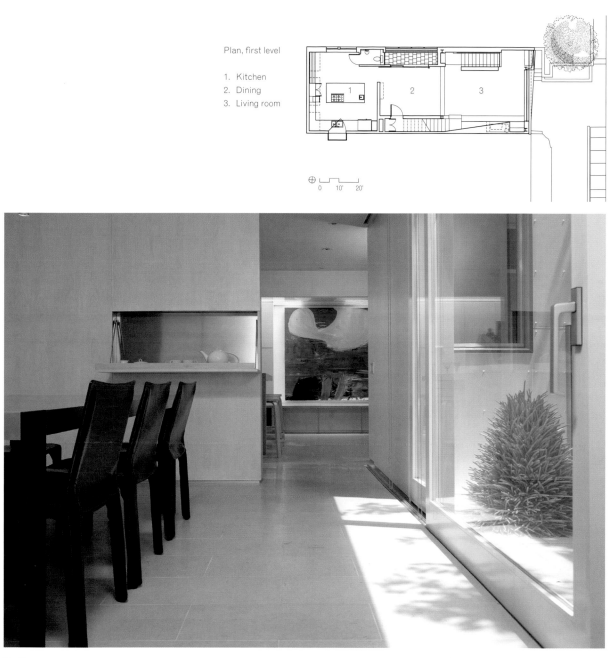

Section

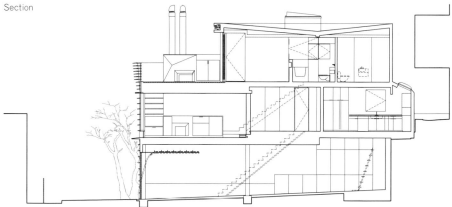

Plan, second level

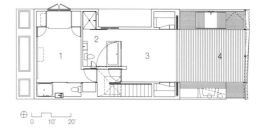

1. Guest suite
2. Master bathroom
3. Master bedroom
4. Roof terrace

Park Presidio Residence

San Francisco

Located in an urban residential area adjacent to San Francisco's Park Presidio, the private residence sits between city grid and open space. The client's extensive collection of large-scale contemporary photography informed the spatial organization of the house, intertwining formal and informal vertical circulation with gallery exhibition.

The plaster and glass facade is objectified, overhanging the slope of the entry. Vehicular access parallels the front door, bifurcated by an auto ramp to the garage and a metal entry bridge to the front door. The bridge extends the urban streetscape with the material, dimension, and language of the sidewalk, pulling it deep within the interior to define the public quality of the gallery. The ramp, or drivescape, deforms the surface of street, quoting tree grates, street drains, and utility covers. This unprecedented arrangement of entry and domain subverts traditional demarcations between public and private, rescripting the relationship of infrastructure and dwelling.

The fully self-sufficient energy system sustaining the house integrates programmatic and tectonic strategies to augment its environmental performance. The roof surface supports a field of crystalline silicon photovoltaic modules incorporating a 150-square-foot skylight of photovoltaic laminated glass and amorphous cellular technology. The four-story stairwell beneath the skylight benefits, illuminating its translucent handrail surfaces from the top-floor master bedroom suite to the ground floor entry foyer.

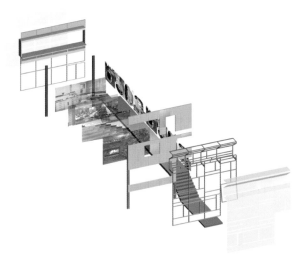

Exploded axonometric, ground level sequence

Site plan

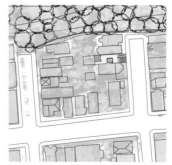

Plan, first level

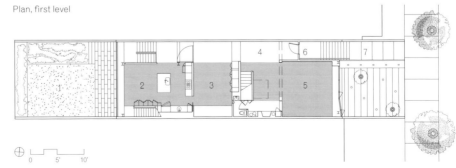

1. Rear-yard garden
2. Kitchen
3. Dining
4. Gallery
5. Living
6. Entry
7. Site entry

0   5'   10'

Section

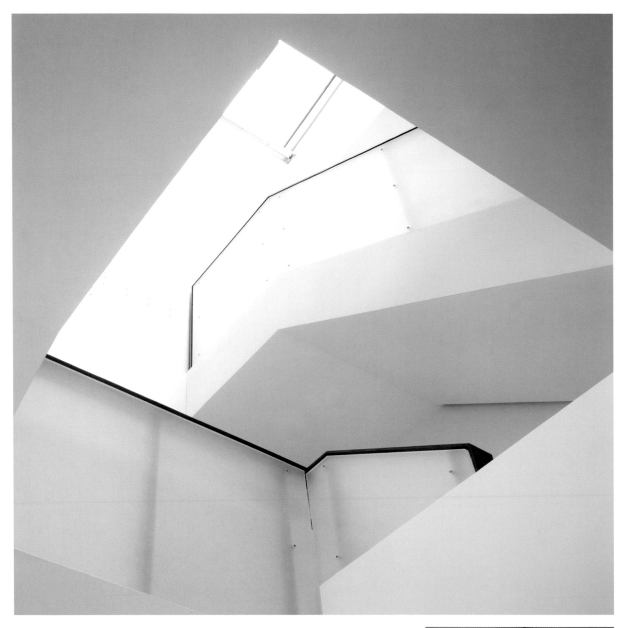

Russian Hill Penthouse

San Francisco

Expansive views to the bay distinguish this 1960s tower at the eastern edge of Russian Hill. Ephemeral conditions of landscape are internalized in this penthouse residence, informing its articulation and materiality. Vistas of the city, the bay, Golden Gate Bridge, Alcatraz Island, and surrounding mountains unfold in all directions, continually transformed by environmental factors of fog, tide, and sunlight. The elongated proportions of the floor-plate are coordinated with the organization of program, controlling the sequence to both discover and experience the view. Domestic functions inform the strategy to establish relationships with the specific landscapes they foreground.

The planning and detailed surfaces are designed to establish seamless continuity with environmental context beyond the window. A translucent glass wall blade bifurcates the space on entry, offering dual tangential paths toward the living area. The gesture is further defined through subtle shifts and inflections in both plan and section, freeing the interior from the perimeter walls to relay formal and material qualities of the distant natural surfaces. The supporting material palette—book-matched cherry, bleached maple, honed limestone, Brazilian granite, and alabaster—collectively coincides with the surrounding environment. Detailed intersections of material and function defer to their position within a larger system of surface.

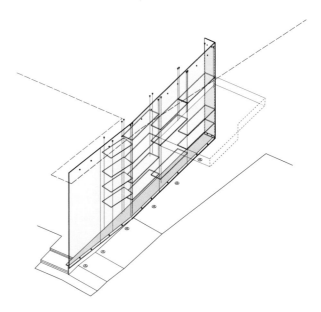

Axonometric, glass blade at entry

Site plan, city

29   Russian Hill Penthouse

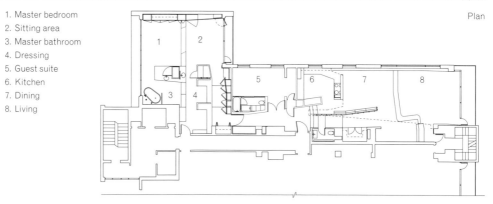

1. Master bedroom
2. Sitting area
3. Master bathroom
4. Dressing
5. Guest suite
6. Kitchen
7. Dining
8. Living

Plan

0   5'   10'

William Wurster Renovation

San Francisco

The renovation of a four-level urban courtyard house, designed by William Wurster in 1960, establishes new relationships to its context and explores issues of programmatic specificity. The project's strategic modifications to the existing envelope enrich the visual connections between its interiors and the city, bay, and distant landscapes. The original organization and volume were also adjusted to invigorate the courtyard adjacencies, with a focus on internalizing views. Broad new expanses of the horizon are now balanced with intimate connections to the entry garden. The urban form, image, and materiality of the building remain consistent with the original design; however, a finer grain of articulation, a sensual material palette,

and traces of programming have been added to the discourse of Wurster's modernist vocabulary.

A series of program-specific interventions are brought in to initiate relationships between the living spaces and functional cores. The plans are adjusted to enrich and destabilize the distinct boundaries of the existing and undifferentiated white rooms; the circulation is now continuous, flexible, and responsive to spaces, engaging contemporary patterns of dwelling and working. Functions overlap one another and are expressed through subtle shifts in material and detail along a contiguous system of operable storage and flexible partitions that fold, slide, and interlock, offering a subtle change in persona and latent evidence of use.

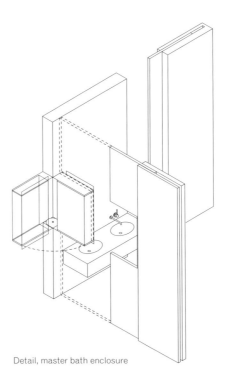

Detail, master bath enclosure

FRAGMENT/hinge: In alliance with its modern predecessor, details are born from formal rather than linguistic acts—transformations invoked to obscure the transparency of banal signifiers in an effort to intensify perception and furnish material and spatial continuities between distinct artifacts. The detail becomes the filter through which architecture is experienced, where the fragment, in its multiplicity, refers back to the larger complexity of the whole. The hybrid element, such as the hinged fragment conflating wall, door, window, and wardrobe, blocks signification at the outset while theatricalizing those spatial acts—cut, shift, rotate—that engender the making of both separation and aperture and that qualify, although through a paradoxical splitting, their very meaning and genesis.
–I. B.

Plan, entry level

1. Studio
2. Entry
3. Courtyard
4. Guest suite

0 5' 10'

Section

Hillsborough Residence

Hillsborough, California

Rescripting key tenets of the modernist orthodoxy is at the heart of the redesign of a residence located in a suburban context south of San Francisco. Designed by Jim Nagle of Nagle Hartray Architects in 1980, the house was conceived in the Chicago-modernist tradition. The goal of the redesign was to introduce incidences of specificity sponsored by program and site, setting up a deflection of the overriding universality of space and materials.

In dialogue with the original strategy, the thresholds of site, garden, and dwelling are restated as lingering and fluid overlaps that incorporate the matured landscape and gentle climate. Blades of Corten steel carve a pathway through a screen of oaks to the main entry. Arrival is marked by the congregation of autonomous garden and building elements, each with its own unique materiality. A canopy of translucent glass rests on a plinth of integral colored concrete nested into a retaining wall, also of Corten steel. A placid water feature reflects the dappled light of the canopy on a watery plinth of black polished concrete.

Selected zones throughout the home are delineated by materials and configuration specific to their use. New window and wall systems introduce a blurring of indoor and outdoor spaces, and domestic elements become sculptural moments in this expanded field. Rearticulating spaces throughout constituted a strategic palette of surfaces, writing a new narrative of materiality.

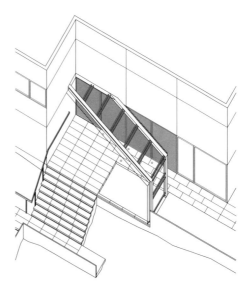

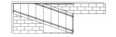

Axonometric, entry canopy

Site plan, immediate context

Plan

1. Pool
2. Family room
3. Entry
4. Garden
5. Living
6. Dining
7. Garage
8. Breakfast

Private Residence and LEF Foundation Offices / Gallery, in Collaboration with Jim Jennings Architecture

Napa Valley, California

An existing stone structure is converted for dual uses as a private residence and as offices and gallery for the LEF Foundation. The stone enclosure, built in the 1880s, offered a context that is pure and iconic in its space and monolithic in its construction. To maintain the plan's purity and openness, the program was divided into a series of autonomous systems that float freely, resisting and preserving the perimeter walls.

The ground-floor gallery/offices are designed as a series of nomadic storage units and movable exhibition panels, allowing flexibility in use. The mobile cabinets glide along tracks embedded in the floor and may be reconfigured as needed to accommodate a diversity of programs: library, exhibit, office, and conference. Echoing the evident assembly of the historic stone shell, the walls, cabinetry, and systems are designed to portray their essential construction, establishing a resonance between old and new.

The upper-floor residence is dictated by a similar strategy. Anchored by a system of interdependent walls and enclosures that contain the domestic functions, its partitions are arranged in an open plan to preserve and free the contiguous surface of the stone enclosure. A concrete tower addition to the west corner accommodates a salon and library. The form restates the monolithic construction of the stone, standing in dialogue and linked through the communication of its surface and construction.

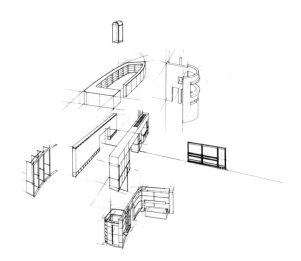

Exploded axonometric of interventions

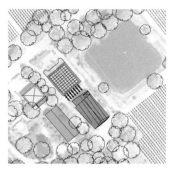

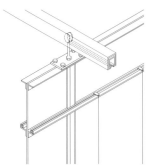

Detail, art display wall at gallery

Plan, ground level

1. Court
2. Entry
3. Residence entry
4. Office / gallery
5. Covered outdoor area
6. Garden library

Detail, library unit at gallery

61 Private Residence and LEF Foundation Offices / Gallery

Section

Plan

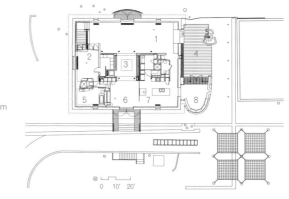

1. Living room
2. Master bedroom
3. Library
4. Deck
5. Master bath
6. Dining
7. Kitchen
8. Salon

0 10' 20'

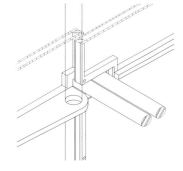

Detail, master bedroom, east wall

Plan, nest (third)

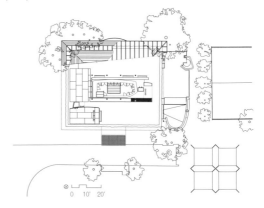

0   10'   20'

Detail, skylight

Guesthouse / Gallery

Nob Hill, San Francisco

The project is designed as choreography of intentional friction between the identity of the domestic and the space of display. This strategy differentiates the building's perimeter walls as display surfaces for art and compresses domestic functions—lounging, entertaining, resting, and bathing—into hybridized objects whose forms, images, and scale challenge their role and relationship to the building.

The discrete programs are furniture-like, each given a distinct portraiture and face. A bench of upholstered industrial felt serves as the main seating for the living area but whose back drapes to cover an entire room on the floor below. The tautly stretched fabric is a tectonic surface, whose patterning and assembly introduce indeterminacy to its scale. The two domestic cores are objectified, enmeshing sleeping, bathing, cooking, and dressing. Repetitive images of rendered drapery are wallpapered over the firm and complex surfaces, blurring their edges of programmatic distinction.

The building's exterior skin extends the exploration of thick surface, an assembly of translucent corrugated panels that both reveal and veil its structure and overscaled roof skylight beneath. The building is a companion to the Nob Hill Residence, stretching out as the foreground to the view toward the Golden Gate Bridge and San Francisco Bay.

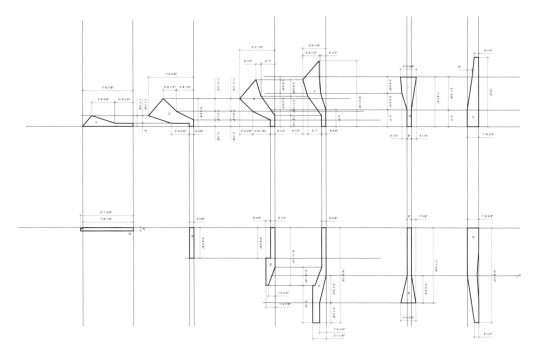

Detail, upholstery patterns

Plan, roof

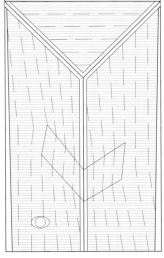

Site plan, immediate context

Section

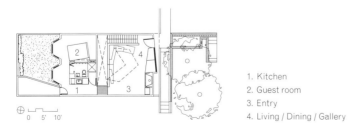

1. Kitchen
2. Guest room
3. Entry
4. Living / Dining / Gallery

0 5' 10'

FOLD/pleat: The body finds its extension in the skin-clothing-cladding continuum, as the layering of upholstered surfaces—both simulated and real—dismantle the objective optical ordering of interior space. The fold is a device of transformation, finding spatiality in the serial undulations and shifting inclinations that cut across the horizontal and vertical delineations of space. The fold of a stair, pleat of a surface detail, undulation

of upholstery, and sensory pulse of a digital image are simultaneously linked and differentiated by degrees of contiguity, tone, and inflection—providing continuities and discontinuities that traverse material and spatial distinctions as they gather and disperse in relation to each other.

–I. B.

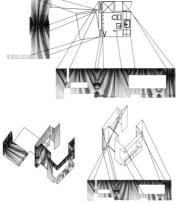

Diagram, digital imagery over upstairs core

Plan, lower level

0   5'   10'

1. Garden
2. Bedroom
3. Bathroom
4. Workroom

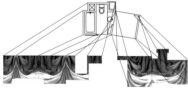

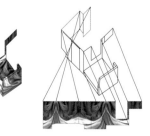

Diagram, digital imagery over downstairs core

Lodi Bunkhouse

St. Helena, California

Situated on a vineyard in the flatlands of the Napa Valley, the project's narrow parcel parallels the Napa River and abandoned Southern Pacific rail line. The bunkhouse's planning, fenestration, and assembly reverberate with the site's inherent orders of directionality and scale. Functioning as an artist's retreat, the program includes open studios, communal domestic zones, and individual bunkrooms.

The organization is dominated by a continuous central void running the length of the shed to connect the interior with two distinct landscapes: a grove of hawthorn trees to the north and vineyards to the south. Additionally, the space is a circulator, sponsoring flexible and fluid patterns of inhabitation, use, and activity. The thickening of the building envelope, with its exterior membrane of semitransparent fiberglass, reveals a sublayered network of structure, fenestration, and sheathing. Its rectangular apertures are regularized in an offset pattern, dispersing filtered sunlight by day and emitting a luminous pattern by night.

The front facade fully opens; airplane hangar industrial doors to the north and garage door systems to the south take advantage of the prevailing summer winds and passively cool the thermal mass of the concrete base. The structural approach is integrated with both passive and active environmental systems, such as heating water through a piped solar-system between the structural plywood sheathing and the exterior's semitransparent corrugated skin. The extended shade canopy to the south also supports an array of photovoltaic cells, providing for the building's energy requirements.

Exploded axonometric

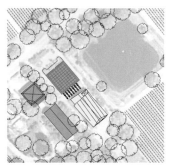

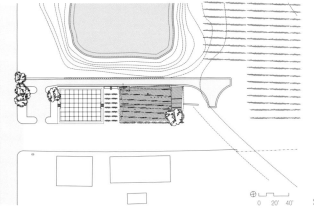

0   20'   40'   Site plan

Plan

1. Kitchen / Dining
2. Living
3. Bunkroom
4. Central Void
5. South Canopy
6. Entry
7. Studio
8. Guest apartment

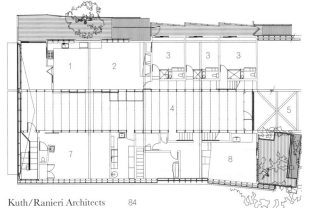

Kuth/Ranieri Architects   84

0   5'   10'

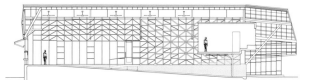

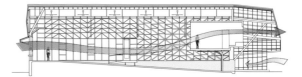

Thermal section

Diagrammatic elevation

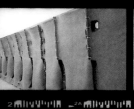

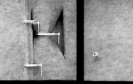

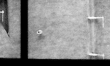

Kuth/Ranieri's Performance of Modernism

Mitchell Schwarzer

In the built work of Kuth/Ranieri Architects, the frankness of modern design is complemented by a determination for the sensuality of form. Byron Kuth and Elizabeth Ranieri, the firm's founding principals, might be called neomodernists. They adhere to modern architecture's rigorous expression of structure and function as well as its refusal of ornament. At the same time, their urge to bring modern materials and building systems out of industrial austerity leads them to heighten the drama. Their architectural frame sprouts sculptural appendages. Walls cast and transgress boundaries. Furniture occupies space and participates as both infrastructure and circulation. Glazing thickens and complicates the passage of light and sight. Program performs.

It is no accident that working artists and art collectors in the San Francisco Bay Area have been drawn to Kuth/Ranieri. The landscape is notable for its dramatic scale and fluidity. Here, the sun burns brightly. Steep slopes constantly shift point of view. So, too, the populace seems afflicted by an ethereal, centrifugal energy, a pulling apart of rule and role. Kuth/Ranieri's work, poised on the precipice of recognition and distortion, fits its context.

During the late 1980s, many local artists and architects were vigorously engaging materials. There were the performances of Survival Research Laboratory, founded by Mark Pauline in 1978. The San Francisco group redirected remains of military and industrial technology into critique and spectacle under banner titles like *The Deliberate Destruction of Elaborately Engineered Artifacts*.

A closer architectural influence was David Ireland's Capp Street Project, which started out in 1975. Ireland had purchased a Victorian in San Francisco's Mission District. He stripped wallpaper. He ripped off window moldings. He chucked the furniture but kept a television set, a broom, and some bent wire. He then coated walls, floors, and remaining bric-a-brac with glossy polyurethane. The house glowed like an insect trapped in amber. Ireland showed how the character of place owes much to the pliable nature of surface, how the removal or encasement of history's layers can change appearance.

Along with Ireland, other Bay Area architects and artists working in the late 1980s were interested in the repurposing of materials and functions. The Marin Headlands Center for the Arts (a former military base in Marin County) sponsored projects and installations by Bruce Tomb and John Randolph (IOOA), Ann Hamilton, and Mel

Chin, as well as Ireland. The work demonstrated to Kuth and Ranieri the power of raw materials and the possibility for engendering wonder by programmatically redirecting their physicality.

The devastating 1989 Loma Prieta earthquake changed the landscape of the Bay Area region, bringing young firms the opportunity to build. When a nineteenth-century stone building that housed offices for LEF Foundation was badly damaged in the quake, the foundation hired the new firm of Kuth/Ranieri Architects to design its offices and gallery as well as renovate an attached private residence. The architects added a curved concrete tower to the existing structure; otherwise, they left its stone walls intact. Within the interior, they built a series of furniture units that glide on tracks embedded in the floor. The program floated freely in space. Depending on need, the space could be rearranged for use as offices, a conference room, a gallery, or a library. Instead of a room with furniture in it, the LEF Foundation offices resembled a rail yard where "boxcars" await their turn to switch position.

Like the LEF Foundation building, in which furniture plays an architectural role beyond its program, the architects further explored these ideas for a guesthouse on San Francisco's Nob Hill. The architects had taken the idea of programmatic disruption of space to the point where a single functional element nearly consumes an entire building. The clients had earlier commissioned Kuth/Ranieri to design their house, across the small alley, on the basis of the architects' installation at the San Francisco Museum of Modern Art. *Fabrications* (1998) embedded felt seating into a wall, creating a soft garment titled "Body in Repose." Kuth/Ranieri extended this investigation of the rapport between bodies and buildings to the scale of a single-family house. A 25-foot-long, L-shaped banquette made of felt energizes the entire public space, acting as both seating and wall. Its back cascades down to the lower level, engaging the stairs and confusing the solidity of wall with the folds of fabric, the sureness of steps with the softness of seating.

The client's main residence, completed in 2000, shows similar motivations, yet ones expressed on the facade. Kuth/Ranieri were interested in expanding the customary choices given to an architect in designing a row house facade. Neither the modernist attitude of expressing only functions like the modulation of light or the circulation of people nor the historicist and postmodernist approach of adding contextual maneuvers and period ornaments was acceptable. In San Francisco, the latter approach was almost the letter of law. Residential Design Guidelines of the city's Planning Department push architects to incorporate as many traditional features as possible: wood facing, bay windows, a terminating cornice. The challenge for the Nob Hill Residence was to design a composition that would incorporate San Francisco's Victorian and Edwardian traditions while breaking new ground.

Kuth/Ranieri first abstracted the key functional elements that made up the facade—the apertures through which people and automobiles, light and views move, as well as the cladding alongside those apertures. They then laid out a grid across the entire facade that incorporated each of the elements and changed dimension and projection from bottom to top; the grid narrows as it moves upward, and its slats project farther out as they ascend. Subsequently, the architects situated the functional elements within the grid, intentionally confusing their materiality with that of the overall mahogany cladding system. Since the garage door is flush with the facade surface, the architects were able to harmonize automobile egress with the entire composition.

At the other extreme, they employed a visible steel I-beam to support a large central plate-glass window—a blatant departure from older houses in the city. Kuth/Ranieri ameliorated this bold gesture by placing an interpretation of the traditional bay window alongside the plate-glass window, providing a continuity of glass across the width of the facade. It does not protrude so much from the facade as it rolls forward. Finally, instead of tacking on a gratuitous cornice, the architects concluded the building by narrowing and projecting the grid as a parapet alongside the roof deck. And, because the house is approached obliquely, changes in the grid yield a sense of fluid movement. In this Nob Hill house, Kuth/Ranieri crafted a thoroughly contemporary building whose earthen-brown color and finely honed details mesh with the lush flora and older buildings alongside it.

Kuth/Ranieri's lyrical talents come to full fruition at the Lodi Bunkhouse, again in the Napa Valley and once more with the LEF Foundation as client. Like most of their work, this building was an exhaustive renovation of an older structure. At a vineyard site between an abandoned rail line and the Napa River, the program included dining, living, and meeting rooms, as well as bedrooms for artists. Wanting to express the new use of the shed and still fit into the rich agricultural valley, the architects chose to veil the building's perimeter: a provocation intended to prompt curiosity about its use. Ranieri remarks that when you drive up to Napa, you notice that the old agrarian buildings have slightly distorted shapes, deformed by their programs to cover feed or provide shade for animals. They're very specific, yet abstract at the same time. Similarly, Kuth/Ranieri wanted its building to evoke a chain of reactions. The building's belonging to the landscape went much further than mimicking existing natural or built forms. It was a matter of setting the stage for architecture to tell a story.

Architectural inspiration for the project came from near and far. Like the Berkeley-based 1960s firm MLTW (Kuth worked for partner Charles Moore in the early 1980s), Kuth and Ranieri were inspired by the astounding shapes of agrarian architecture in Northern California. And like MLTW's epochal Sea Ranch, the bunkhouse's unusual shape merges vernacular research with artistic inspiration. Nonetheless, instead of cladding their structure in wood and shutting it off from further inspection, the architects wanted to provoke the public by revealing perceptual depth through the skin and into the building's systems.

Approaching the bunkhouse, observers note that the translucent fiberglass exoskeleton reinforces the shed's agrarian appearance and also hints at its new use. At moments, the building harmoniously rises into its landscape, with the limbs of trees even poking out of a wooden deck. Still, the translucent skin discloses more than the wooden boards cladding older buildings nearby. Viewers see through the bunkhouse to the grid of wooden supports, which alludes to the rapport between skin and structure. At night, when the building is illuminated, visitors can see from the outside the fuzzy patterns of people moving within—the skin acting like a filter on a camera lens as the chalk-colored exoskeleton modulates vision in and out of focus.

The main egress is provided at both front and back through airplane-hangar-like doors that can be drawn open or shut, to reveal or conceal the interior. At one side, long industrial windows similarly open and close, changing the bunkhouse's overall shape and connecting it with the outdoors. Inside, the architects continued their exploration of how surface can intrude into, intermingle with, and shape space. To allow light to penetrate deep into the central void, they designed a 90-foot wall of open-lattice trusses. Likewise, infrastructure fills the large space; mechanical, plumbing, electrical, lighting, and seismic systems are exposed.

At the beginning of the twenty-first century, in the midst of the Information Age, Kuth/Ranieri Architects are attempting a merger of industry and information. For them, architecture must not merely provide a programmatic space supported by underlying and often invisible systems. It must also use the systems as occasions for developing ideas. A century ago, Bay Area architects such as Bernard Maybeck and Ernest Coxhead had a similar notion. Yet they focused largely on engaging the public's attention with how the structural materials of their time fit together to make space. Today, in this technologically advanced age, Kuth/Ranieri have extended that quest to the broader arena of creating highly tuned sensory environments. How, they ask, can a building invite its users and viewers to a performance of its structural loads, its cladding, its lighting, its heating and cooling, its provision of not just plumbing and electricity but also electronic transmission, its division of space into work and play areas, zones of public access and privacy? How far, their Lodi Bunkhouse asks, can a building be stripped down, so that passersby are titillated by the wonder of what's revealed—and what's not?

In interiors, in city houses, and in arts centers, Kuth/Ranieri's work takes on the idiosyncratic landscape and culture of Northern California. Their architecture celebrates the intricacy of nature and the tradition, reaching back to the Arts and Crafts Movement, of expressing its charms in precision joinery and textured materials. Wherever they build, the architects press into context. Their facades intertwine with the gardens of a San Francisco alley and the riparian ecosystem along the Napa River, and provide a lustrous canvas for reflecting the region's powerful light. Their interiors make use of large windows to break walls open to long vistas, and become the stage for another trip altogether—space contorted by the nomadic maneuvers of furniture, space molded by the material character of those enigmatic partitions.

When Kuth/Ranieri Architects wield architecture as an instrument of communication, they do so by giving full attention to how architecture can advance experience and memory. They are regionalists, to the extent that they are interested in using their buildings as situations from which stories will be revealed over time— stories that will point to present-day realities as well as older patterns. An architectural intervention, in this sense, belongs to place, not merely by attending to it and borrowing from it. Rather, architecture must offer something back. It must capture and amplify, with its own devices, the minutely specific and infinitely numerous moments when human bodies interact with the material riches of the environment.

No Obstacles: Notes on Martyrs' Square and Other Roofscapes

Rodolphe el-Khoury

The roof occupies a relatively modest position in contemporary architectural theory. While plan, elevation, and section have their advocates and continue to provoke debates on their role and status in the production of architecture, few if any argue on behalf of the roof or a reflected ceiling plan. The roof does crop up in recurrent debates on style where the traditionalist commitment to the vernacular is pitted against the ahistorical rationalism of modernist architecture. Without fail, the emphasis in such discussions is on iconography—flat versus pitched roofs—and the issues debated are relevant only to residential architecture.[1] Roofs still make grand architectural statements in houses, but they are practically invisible in large institutional buildings and are usually reserved for back-of-the-house functions as well as mechanical equipment.[2] Yet the changing attitude toward environmental controls and their dedicated infrastructure may lately be pulling the roof into greater visibility. The roof is increasingly valued, not merely as a repository for expensive air-conditioning machinery but most importantly as a solar interface.

What follows is a commentary on projects by Kuth/Ranieri Architects in which roofs take center stage.[3] They serve critical functions in regulating and sustaining comfort zones within and around buildings, yet they also have structuring roles on many levels and in many aspects of architecture, both symbolic and performative. A prime example of roof architecture, the Martyrs' Square project, pushes to an extreme certain latent tendencies that are partially and intermittently manifested in Kuth/Ranieri's work.

The Martyrs' Square project, submitted to an international competition in Beirut, Lebanon, proposes a new vision for the historic site, including a detailed program for the urban surface and underground. The project's centerpiece is an oversized canopy that extends from the heart of the city to its northern waterfront.

The competition called for the rebuilding of the existing venerated square—the epicenter of the old capital—as well as the surrounding blocks. It would be a landmark project in the ongoing reconstruction of the city center after Lebanon's protracted civil war. The vast site had been prepared for development: bulldozed, excavated, leveled, and serviced. As one of the most important developing areas in the city, it had also recently gained global notoriety because of widely circulated photographs and news reports showing immense crowds covering the entire field. It was this massive public demonstration that precipitated radical changes in the country.

With images of the oceanic crowd blanketing the open field fresh in mind, the burden of architectural responsibility weighed on every line of the proposal— delineating (and confining) the public realm. Therefore, bringing development to the site and giving definitive shape to the square became a difficult proposition in this physical and political context.

Growth in Beirut's business district is inevitable and indeed necessary for financing the reconstruction process. Yet development of this site, which had just enabled the most potent transformative act in the city's recent history, risked a troubling, but perhaps avoidable, problem: the physical and regulatory compartmentalization of the unobstructed open field into discrete areas. Any partitioning of the area through design, indeed any differentiation of the ground at all, could compromise the freedoms that this open field promised with every unscripted public event.

In lieu of a comprehensive master plan, the Martyrs' Square project proposed flexible strategies for the occupation of the ground and a single, albeit gigantic, object: a roof structure stretching from one end of the site to the other. The roof was designed in detail, while features of landscape and urban design were left open to interpretation and change. The roof is a finite, concrete object. It was to be built gradually in phases that anticipated the waves of development, though the form was set and precisely described. Other aspects of the project were meant to evolve through open-ended processes that invited public participation and welcomed unexpected outcomes.

The roof structure consists mainly of rectangular corrugated metal panels that are tessellated in finely orchestrated patterns and supported on slender, treelike columns. The roof extends along the central axis of the site in a continuous strip of varying width. It covers the entire original square, narrows to a thin canopy to shade a path along an archaeological site farther north, and reemerges in its full magnitude as a roof for a ferry terminal. It shelters a variety of programs but also serves as a unifying formal element that ties various episodes into an urban sequence extending deep into the city. The pattern of the roof tiles changes continuously, shifting back and forth from precise regularity to turbulent disarray. Moments of calm order coincide with programmed amenities that benefit from optimized and sustained protection, whether in the heat or the rain. Turbulence erupts most dramatically around the existing Martyrs' monument, disrupting the roof's programmatic and environmental logic to expose the charged ground to the open sky.

With flocking panels that glide above the square and only occasionally touch down in fleeting contact with the ground, the project is ostensibly at odds with current preoccupations in architecture and the pervasive investment in landscape. The ground, though typically central to Kuth/Ranieri Architects' projects in its multiple layers and complex ecology, here becomes secondary to a superstructure that is persistently and deliberately detached from the landscape. While trendsetting buildings such as Foreign Office Architect's Yokohama Ferry Terminal reached unprecedented extremes in integrating building and ground, thus transforming architecture into a built landscape, in Martyrs' Square the roof and ground remain physically, if not functionally, separate.

We may see in Martyrs' Square—and in several other projects from the Kuth/Ranieri Architects and ReK Productions team—an exception to an otherwise consistent dedication to landscape and its capacity to immerse the architectural object in the vital currents that traverse the city. More relevant yet is to recognize common theoretical threads that align the roofscape of Martyrs' Square with the logic of landscape. The common genealogy in which the stubborn fixity of architecture is pitted against the informal, dynamic process it contains should clarify the ideas behind roofscapes and their place in the current architectural debate.

The common thread is a persistent philosophical theme that found its most ambitious formulation with Jean-Jacques Rousseau. In 1755 Rousseau became an overnight sensation with the publication of the *Discourse on the Origin and Basis of Inequality Among Men,* in which he outlined the main themes of his political philosophy. He singles out one foundational act in a mythical history of decline that accounts for many of civil society's ills: the building of the first fence. The wall (that is, architecture) is what separates and excludes. It lies at the root of discrimination and repression among peoples. Rousseau's antipathy toward architecture, the artificial obstacle to free-flowing interaction and communion among human beings, sharpens in his critique of the theater. The festival, the countermodel he describes, stands as pure presence, a performance that undermines the distinction between spectator and spectacle, spectator and spectator, to achieve an unmediated communion of souls in an obstacle-free environment.

As a frame to the spectacle—an agent of the structural separation between subject and object—architecture stands as a paradigm of mediation. The obstructive compartments of its exclusive interiors erect still more barriers to collective communion. In its sheer materiality, as an opaque object in an open landscape, architecture is the obstacle to the utopia that Rousseau yearns for but can only glimpse in the momentary freedom of the free-flowing and unwalled festival.

Rousseau's metaphors of the festival resurface, almost intact, in British postwar architecture, with the most potent renditions being found in Fun Palace and Archigram's *Instant City*. They are pushed to an absurd extreme in Superstudio's imaginary landscapes where Rousseau's vision climaxes in an epiphany of near-total emptiness. They also prefigure the Situationist project, leading directly to the worlds of artists such as Constant (in his New Babylon world city) and later to the work of the Office for Metropolitan Architecture (OMA).

A closely related thematic may be found at the core of Rem Koolhaas's work, starting with *Delirious New York*. In this iconoclastic reading of Manhattan, architecture comes off as decorative packaging. It is an epiphenomenon and sometimes an obstacle to the economic and social processes that animate the city. Koolhaas followed up this critique with a series of projects that sought a rich orchestration of events within and around buildings. They explored compositional methods that emphasized programmatic relations, advantageous marriages as well as friction that may be provoked by strategic proximities. Instead of defining and delineating use within clearly demarcated compartments, Koolhaas proposed fluid programs on magmalike surfaces, seamlessly linking buildings and urban spaces. In a competition project for the Jussieu Library, the ubiquitous surface spirals up several levels to constitute a vertical landscape, serving as a potent model for much of the ramp-based architectures of the last decade. These range from literal translations of buildings into horizontal fields with seamlessly shifting programs to more rhetorically driven versions where the idea of a continuous ground surface is captured in a formal style, as evidenced in Diller + Scofidio and Renfro's Institute of Contemporary Art in Boston.

The impulse behind the dispersal of the autonomous architectural object, and more specifically the immovable vertical wall, into a horizontal field is also what motivates the roofscapes of Martyrs' Square in Beirut, the Malama Learning Center in Hawaii, and the Museum of Contemporary Art at the Luther Burbank Center for the Arts in Santa Rosa, California (MOCA).[4] These projects invest in the roof—a surface customarily hidden from view and reserved for mechanical equipment—as a primary material, an infrastructural and symbolic means to both enable and enrich life on the ground. The roof constitutes all that is solid and permanent. It supports, frames, modulates, and shelters activities below that are accommodated in less-formal arrangements. In Beirut, the ground plane is crisscrossed by complex, ever-changing activities that the sheltering roof facilitates and channels, rather than fixes or regiments. In Malama, the facilities under the roofscape are designed to adapt easily to the vicissitudes of the site and the institution; they are economical and generic wood-frame structures that can be repeatedly reconfigured for evolving scenarios of inhabitation. In short, the roofscapes in these proposals are inverted landscapes that organize the forces let loose on the ground.

While these projects invite an ad hoc and opportunistic occupation of the ground, they are anything *but* casual in the meticulous design and precise calibration of their roofs. Each roofscape thus comes to most effectively realize the project's representational ambitions. It presents a differentiated yet unified figure that can readily stand as an image-able symbol for the complex aspirations and constituencies of today's institutions.[5] As a piece of infrastructure that performs critical functions in the project's environmental program, the roofscape is also revealed as a demonstration of civic and institutional processes at work. Given Kuth/Ranieri's environmental commitments, capitalizing on the roof—the building's primary solar face—as a site for architectural expression and innovation is a logical and defining move. The roofscape radicalizes a general tendency in their work that recognizes and capitalizes on the performative and figurative potential of the underutilized roof-plane.

The roof as a charged locus of architectural content points back to canonical works by Ludwig Mies Van der Rohe that generally sought to distill building into a question of roof structure. Colin Rowe described the National Gallery in Berlin as a flat dome, underscoring the rhetorical charge carried in the articulation of the exquisite flat roof. The cosmic reference aptly captures the transcendent quality in the classical perfection and universal resonance of Mies's roof. In sharp contrast, Beirut's roofscape is intently caught in the particular; its aspirations are decidedly earthbound.

The National Gallery seems to address its chaotic surrounding with calm indifference. In its tenuous connection with the landscape, Beirut's roofscape seeks to minimize interference with the action on the ground. Detachment here entails a subordination both to site and to the informal processes of everyday life.

As an autonomous object with a hermetic organizational and structural logic, the National Gallery presents a neutral backdrop to events unfolding separately below. The roofscape is a responsive structure that enters into dialogue with its surroundings, adjusting to the dynamics of the site that it seeks to influence and by which it is inflected.

The Convention Hall in Chicago is perhaps Mies Van der Rohe's most radical project in the architecture-as-roof vein. Mies's famous collage, which condenses the architecture into two opposite horizontal fields (a relentlessly consistent space-frame above and a teeming crowd below), invites a comparison with Martyrs' Square. The two should sharpen the difference between a modernist conception of the building as an abstract universal frame with an optimized structure and the roofscape's symbolic and performative ambition: a localized and efficient architecture of differentiated parts that is enmeshed in the site's social and material ecology.

The sinuous contour and intricately variegated form of Martyrs' Square contrast with the regularity of Mies's clearly delineated roof. They are inflected by the fuzzy logic of myriad external influences (natural and artificial) that continuously perturb its geometry. There is no indication of an exterior in Mies's collage. The only element that is *other* than building—that is, the crowd—is molded into the shape of a building: a perfect square.

Individual panels, tiled in shifting patterns, constitute the roofscape. It is a continuous surface formed by the aggregation of singular and highly individuated parts. Unlike Mies's space-frame in which the standardized and mass-produced homogeneity of the constituent parts reinforces the structure's monolithic character—a totality whose individual parts are entirely subordinated to the overwhelming regularity of the whole—the constituent parts of the Martyrs' Square roofscape maintain their autonomy and identity with respect to the whole. They are highly differentiated, mass-customized elements. Each tile is a unique computer-designed and -manufactured product; all come together to constitute a larger figure, bearing inflections that are registered in larger strokes across the whole. The capacity for simultaneous differentiation and conformity allows for nuances in performance and efficiency that respond to local conditions while consolidating action at a larger scale with greater symbolic and environmental ambitions. Given the nature of today's crowds (Beirut's must be a prime example) in which individuals congregate as a "multitude" with shared experiences of alienation rather than as a "people" with a common identity—and considering the complex ecological dynamics that environmentally conscious architects now face at every urban site—the roofscape, as explored in Martyrs' Square, at the Malama Learning Center, and at other projects, is well equipped to take on new challenges and opportunities in the twenty-first-century city.

1 The debate reached a fever pitch in Weimar-era Germany when it resonated with political intentions, dividing the opposing camps along the same lines.

2 Diller + Scofidio and Renfro's Museum of Contemporary Art in Boston provides a good example of the disenchanted roof. The building is attentively detailed, particular care having been lavished on the articulation of the ground. The roof is an entirely different matter: it is treated with utmost indifference and could very well be that of a speculative office building. This attitude toward the roof is typical. The neglect is particularly disturbing here because the crude roof design irremissibly clashes with the sophistication consistently exercised elsewhere.

3 The projects discussed in this essay are products of a collaboration between Kuth/Ranieri Architects and myself, Principal of ReK Productions, on competition projects from 2003 to 2005.

4 A similar impulse drives Kuth/Ranieri's interest in kinetic architectures: movable walls, plus partitions and cabinetry on tracks, allowing users to freely reconfigure their own living spaces. The Lodi Bunkhouse, for instance, features in its external envelope large, operable sections that radically effect the flow of space and people through the building, transforming the central hall into a public street at the touch of a button.

5 Robert Levit links the current architectural interest in differentiated components and populated surfaces to a symbolic impulse that seeks to figure contemporary forms of social organization: "The variable cell, with its looser affiliation to a whole, suggests an analogy to the social world: a world of endlessly diverse individuation marked by a declining willingness or ability of diverse individuals to imagine themselves in relationship to a social whole except through sheer arbitrary assembly." See Robert Levit, "Contemporary Ornament: The Return of the Symbolic Repressed," *Harvard Design Magazine* 28 (Spring/Summer 2008): 70–85.

Industrial Fetish

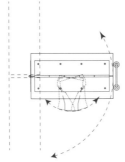
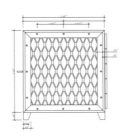

Aluminum, maple, Plexiglas, hair, expanded steel mesh, Peek-O Revolving
Door Viewer, black vinyl, McMaster-Carr hook-and-eye lock
6" × 6" × 3"
San Francisco Museum of Modern Art, Permanent Collection, 1995

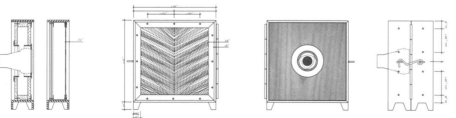

Fabrications: The Body in Repose

800 lb., ½" synthetic felt, 1,000 C-clamps
60' × 7'4" × 20'
San Francisco Museum of Modern Art, Installation February 6–April 28, 1998
Image courtesy SFMOMA

Elevation, interior undershirts

Elevation, exterior jackets

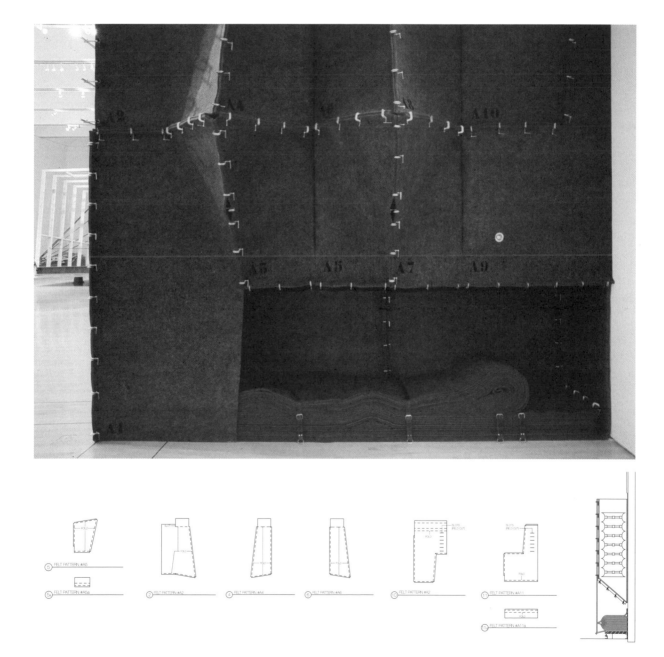

Fields of Fetish: Kuth/Ranieri's Disturbances

Aaron Betsky

Byron Kuth and Elizabeth Ranieri question the white walls that surround us. They question architecture as the production of autonomous buildings, and do so in the making of objects, projects, and built environments. Their work is full of allusion and empty of monumentality. It offers a collage of possibilities and moments of intensities within the blandness of our daily environment, and specifically within the context of the human-made artifices that blanket and suffocate most of the San Francisco Bay Area.

Instead of composing a neutrality of surfaces that give no hint of the structure behind them, Kuth and Ranieri prefer to drape skin and bones loosely over spaces that ramble around from one function, level, or orientation to another. They make loose fits and fetish forms. In their residential and institutional projects, they are in the practice of creating collage lofts: generous assemblies of functional objects in fluid space, defined by both horizontal and vertical skins, always threatening to pull away from each other. This is an effective strategy for constructing flexible places in which we can live and work. In its complexities, it can accommodate the many facets and continual changes of our modern lives. Underlying this manner of working is an attitude toward the nature of architecture as not merely revealing but also making sensible (and sensual) the structures that allow those lives to go on. In so doing, Kuth and Ranieri attempt to destabilize our relation to a neutral reality so that we are forced to come to terms with our corporeal selves and the environment we imprint with our bodies.

Beyond such a practice lies a set of theoretical pursuits. At the core of what these two architects do is fetishization. One of their early works, a theoretically engendered object called *Industrial Fetish*, was emblematic of what they were to do later. It appeared to be an abstracted version of a camera, in which the lens had become a rotating, phallic telescope. It was unclear whether it was looking at the viewer, or whether the viewer was meant to look inside. The box opened up like a book, and a pelt of fake fur covered the inside. Created as part of an exhibition intended to increase AIDS awareness, *Industrial Fetish* combined a kind of heavy-metal aesthetic with overtones of both bondage and the fixation on technology that was central to modernist architecture but with a disturbing sensuality. That almost-sexuality itself integrated the modern tradition of a reliance on (or at least fascination with) the dominance of the visual—a pornography of the hidden, the cleavage where hard surfaces open up to accommodate softness. The object was made with care. Its industrial fasteners, synthetic materials, and geometries sprouting strange anomalies (such as an off-the-shelf door peephole lens) made it clear that these architects were more interested in the latent meaning of materials and their points of connection than in the overall surface. This object also showed the architects' interest in creating distortions. The erotic charge with which they infused this highly manufactured object became central to all their projects, though later it would be much more sublimated.

The most important elaboration of these themes was the project that Kuth and Ranieri created a few years later for an exhibition I curated at the San Francisco Museum of Modern Art (SFMOMA). Called *Fabrications*, it attempted to point to the literal and symbolic fabrications that I believed were central to the making of architecture, by asking architects to strip away the excuses of firmness, commodity, and delight that usually cloaked architecture with building. It did so by commissioning site-specific installations in the museum's largest white-walled gallery space. Kuth and Ranieri's response was to strip away a large portion of one of those towering white walls, replacing it with felt panels held together with rows of C-clamps. Slits in *The Body in Repose*, as they called the piece, provided glimpses of the hidden world inside what most visitors until then had regarded as nothing more than a blank surface on which images (paintings) would appear. The felt took up one entire wall, reaching well above head height and wrapping around the corner. There it went up to the ceiling while providing a small indentation where the visitor could become a body in repose, lying on layers of felt that bunched at one end into a cushion, while another person could sit next to her or him. The situation enacted the standard relationship of a psychiatrist listening to a patient on a couch.

The Body in Repose was a seminal piece of antibuilding architecture. It denied the neutrality of the white wall that serves, in the museum and elsewhere, as a functional backdrop, replacing it instead with something that was sensual and articulate. It was a body in response to our human form, but it was also of a form that made it a version, perhaps the hidden self, of the building—its undergarment. Kuth and Ranieri could have used insulation, which would have been a truer representation of what hides in the wall— yet this was a museum, after all, and thus the architects chose a "high-art" textile that carried allusions, for instance, to Joseph Beuys's use of the same material. The piece also recalled architecture before building, namely, the second skin of clothing that became the tent, a *meuble* version of the *immeuble*. It might even have alluded to the cave out of which we came and which is the place of dreams, not only in psychiatric reversion but also in

Plato's foundational myth for metaphysics. And all this was held together by off-the-shelf hardware (thus asserting the necessity of construction and space making, though not an overall system relating these two).

After these two projects, Kuth and Ranieri have returned only rarely to the making of antibuildings or nonbuildings, preferring instead to install their experiments in their small built projects as well as in proposals for larger constructions. Two notable exceptions were the 2008 project *Folding Water: City of the Future* and the *San Jose Climate Clock*, of the same year. In the former, a submerged artificial barrier reef or dam performs the role of the felt skin, regulating the waters of San Francisco's bay. It turns the surface of the Pacific into a waterfall or vertical surface while also interrupting it with a walkway that lets a viewer observe what was once a datum as a natural, moving phenomenon. In so doing, it also makes the viewer aware of the larger natural forces at work in the ocean while altering the conditions in which they operate. There is a more or less rational result of all this: namely, the creation of a protective barrier to buffer the rise in sea levels because of climate change and the creation of both transportation and urban infrastructure. The main point of the project's design, as opposed to its engineering, is this moment of awareness.

This is even truer in the *Climate Clock* project, a black tower, or aedicule, that Kuth and Ranieri propose constructing out of carbon fiber. The two worked collaboratively on the project with the acclaimed sound artist Bill Fontana. The object is a twisted version of the kind of monumental rotunda whose locus classicus is the Pantheon and whose local version is the freestanding, vestigial Palace of Fine Arts in San Francisco's Marina District. Rather than center the observer and make her or him feel as if she or he is at the center of the universe, this peculiar object turns as it moves up, distorting the viewer's sense of place both inside and in relation to the surrounding world. There is an oculus at the top, but this view of the sky is vestigial; what matters are the sounds and sights from twelve "significant ecological habitats" that the team proposes displaying continually on the twelve piers. The *Climate Clock* object is a baroque commentary on a monument for the digital age. It is a monkey's ladder, not aimed up toward divine enlightenment but out toward a disappearing reality.

These two projects expand Kuth and Ranieri's attitudes toward the function of architecture to an urban and a monumental scale. In the former, they take architecture to the level it probably needs to achieve if it is going to be a relevant part of those social and economic structures that control our lives. That is, the scale and complexity of infrastructure make us realize that, as such, the function of architecture within a constellation of forces is to make us aware that our actions are not neutral, not merely productive, and not seamless. When we operate in our natural environment, we create disturbances in fields, offer new points of attraction, and produce anomalies. It is those latter peculiarities that might best correspond to what we may think of as buildings. In the *Climate Clock* project, Kuth and Ranieri propose a particular function for such coalescing nodes of stimulation, namely, to entrain technology in such a manner that we can focus on the much larger forces we are altering through applying that same artifice.

Like most architects, however, Kuth and Ranieri are not in a position to operate on such a grand scale, although they have continued to work out their notions of architecture through teaching and research. What they instead do day-to-day is attempt to install such speculations in specific situations, mainly of a residential project. Their use of fetishized objects has moved from the statement of autonomous form (in the early LEF Foundation offices in Napa Valley, 1995) to the mere hint of metal, rubber, or honed steel in residential projects that have followed (Nob Hill Residence, Park Presidio Residence, Russian Hill Penthouse). Their refusal to create structure and space that stand in a rational relationship to each other and produce clearly functional areas is most evident in the Lodi Bunkhouse, a dormitory addition to the Foundation offices they created eight years later. There the building's skin becomes a continually shifting and sliding cloak of translucent fiberglass panels and its main interior space a bare concrete nave surrounded by a network of white-painted wood trellises. What a visiting artist does there, what holds which thing up, what begins and ends is unclear, yet all the pieces are articulated with almost insane attention.

Two projects that addressed the legacy of the gay liberation struggle, the AIDS Memorial Grove of 2004 and the Harvey Milk Memorial Car of 2001, continued Kuth and Ranieri's interest in infrastructure, skin, and articulation. In the Harvey Milk Memorial design, the main focus is not actually the public space of the plaza, which is more or less left as it is, but a special streetcar named after Milk that runs up and down San Francisco's Market Street, telling Milk's story inside the train and continually installing his memory in the city he helped transform. Architecture here activates and memorializes, though certainly not with a fixed building. Similarly, the AIDS Memorial Grove proposal neither respects nor makes a public space but weaves a drape of new territory, a collage of both natural and human-made materials. It starts as a bench, interrupts the road, flows over the verge, and cascades down into the heart of the city's grandest park where it becomes not a place of memorial but an interruption now of the natural flows of the park, as AIDS interrupted the flow of human life. These are models for making architecture that moves and transforms, interrupts and articulates.

When Kuth and Ranieri concentrate on fulfilling functions, they still manage to hold on to some of the themes they develop in such "special" projects. They remain fascinated with the idea of architecture consisting of a draped cloak that collects functions underneath it in a loose fit. This cloak becomes a piece of infrastructure that provides shade and identity, as in the Malama Learning Center (Hawaii, 2006) or the cultural district for Beirut in their collaborative proposal with Rodolphe el-Khoury for the repair of Martyrs' Square (2003)—both symbolic of the conception of architecture as the articulation and revelation of a field. It is itself the visible version of a system that allows for the creation of moments of coherence. These then stand as warped mirrors of our bodies, or as fetishes. Underneath or without that skin, in the renovations and projects they build in the Bay Area, Kuth and Ranieri shift and veil; slide and slip; use humble materials that, through intense focus, become highly charged; and generally try to reveal something larger about each project.

They want to escape from the world of making static objects in a hierarchical system. They want to compose synthetic moments, integrate differences into modulated systems. Their concepts are as dense as their architecture, and they fetishize terms as much as their built projects do materials. They also reveal their interest in investigating deformations and making them evident. They suspect and bring forward what is latent within a project, below and within a city—the built reality and the human landscape that we accept and on which they operate. What this is, this monster that causes neat and functional systems to go awry, they do not say. Yet what is revealed, through their collection of works, speaks to us: our human bodies, our fears and hopes, and the very nature of what we make. Their latency is what we do not know, and Kuth and Ranieri's work is to articulate that unknown into a fetish that is architecture.

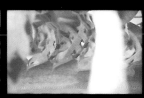

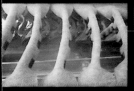

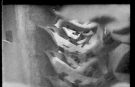

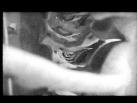

Calistoga House

Calistoga, California

This vacation residence set in California's Napa Valley is designed for a family of five. Situated in the hills above the Silverado Trail, the house commands sweeping vistas of valley and mountains beyond. The courtyard scheme provides an open connection between the interior spaces and surrounding landscape.

The form and construction of the building responds environmentally to the state's larger energy concerns, as well as to the valley's unique and dramatic change in temperature that occurs from day to night. The column and beam structure is made up of precast, pretensioned concrete members, increasing the thermal mass while preserving an open plan and perimeter views. The mass traps the cooler evening temperature, to yield a comfortable daylight environment. The roof's tessellation of spandrels allows daylight to enter the seams of the structure, promoting daylight throughout the interior.

The building's exterior skin is a drape of translucent fiberglass cladding that provides waterproofing, shade, and a ubiquitous diffusion of light. The overall intention of the proposal is to create an environment both contiguous with its landscape and cavelike in its retreat.

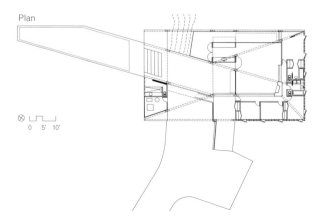

Plan

0   5'   10'

Exploded axonometric

Corrugated fiberglass skin ———————————

Precast concrete joists ———————————

Prestressed concrete
columns / beams ———————————

Ground plane ———————————

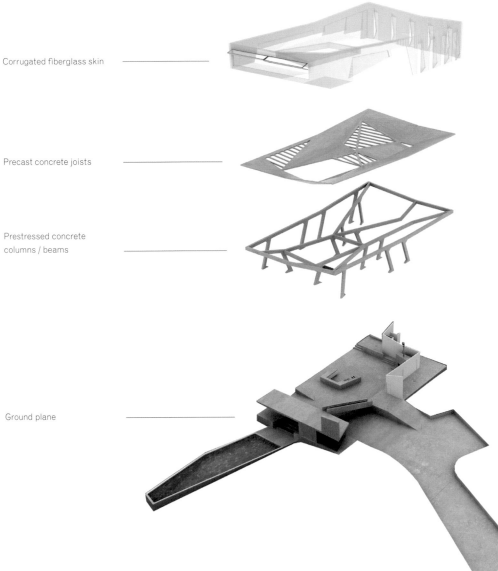

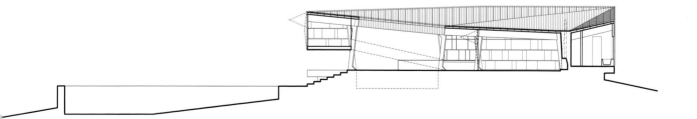

Longitudinal section

Malama Learning Village, in Collaboration with Rodolphe el-Khoury (ReK Productions)

Malama, Hawaii

Central to the strategy of the proposed Learning Village is flexible growth in programming and a sustainable occupation of the project's site. The project integrates three distinct institutional programs under one roof: a high school, a community theater, and a conservation garden. Key design features of canopy and landscape accommodate multiple programs while sustaining a coherent architectural vision rooted in the site's cultural, material, and climatic conditions.

The canopy provides identity as well as shade, regulating sunlight, wind, sound, and water. The steel frame and repetitive roofing panels distort to better perform in particular situations: folding down into a vertical sunshade along the eastern elevation, gently bending into an acoustical shell above the stage, and splaying to modulate light for the agricultural programs. The sawtooth pattern optimizes shading and ventilation while maintaining dramatic views to the mountains and northern sky.

The landscape is organized into distinct territories that converge at the heart of the Learning Village. The alignment of each dedicated program offers opportunities for charged adjacencies. Pedestrian and vehicular entries extend to terraced seating for an open-air theater. And the conservation garden, of native plantings, interfaces with indoor and outdoor classrooms. This open planning minimizes enclosure and eliminates most internal circulation while expanding the public realm of the multidisciplinary campus.

Plan

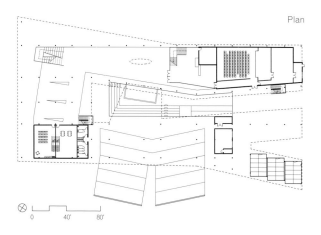

0   40'   80'

Exploded axonometric

Canopy —————————

Structure —————————

Program —————————

Vehicular drop-off —————————

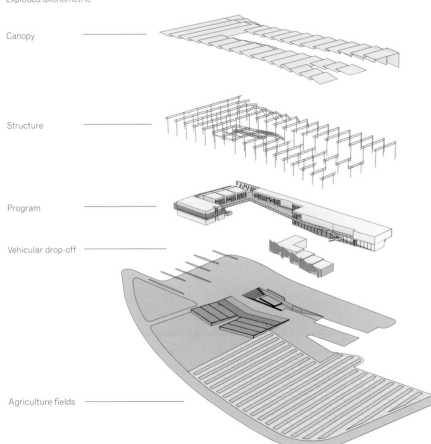

Agriculture fields —————————

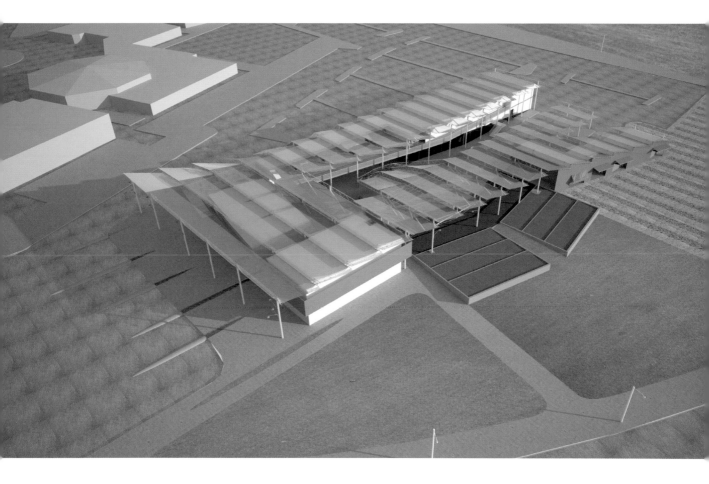

127   Malama Learning Village

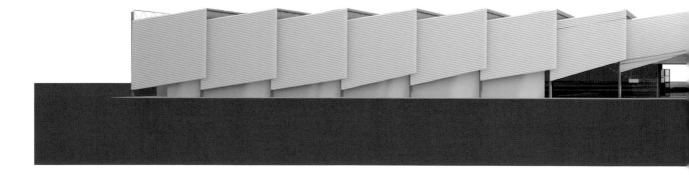

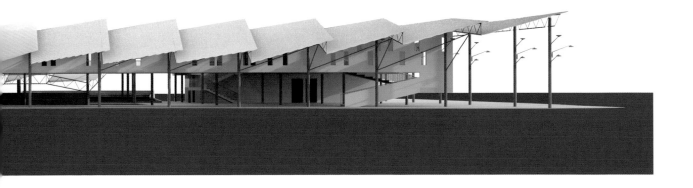

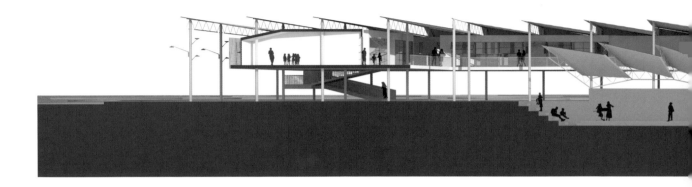

CAMP: A Gateway Proposal for the Contemporary Art Museum Presidio

San Francisco

Located within the National Park Service's Presidio, CAMP is sited at the crest of the Main Post. The iconic and assertive structure frames a broad, open sculpture court flanked by museum galleries. At this Gateway, the new spatial threshold of the CAMP Museum resolves the Parade Ground's monumental spatial corridor while preserving its openness to the natural surroundings.

The project relies on both apparent and latent contextual strategies. Addressing the historic buildings to the east, the flanking walls of the gallery wings are brick, scaled in relationship to the surrounding masonry structures on the Parade Ground. The bunkered plinth draws on the dramatic earthen and concrete gun turrets nestled in the coastal areas of the Presidio.

CAMP promotes a civic engagement with the revitalized cultural and economic life of the Presidio. The image of the institution is envisioned to be both contemporary and timeless, acknowledging the Presidio's history as well as its transformation. The sculpture court, galleries, and educational programs support the interconnectedness between people, place, and work. Taken as an empty figure, the building echoes the abstraction of the museum's typological white wall where contemporary art has the freedom to express itself.

Exploded axonometric

Upper galleries
Entry

Garden
Sculpture court

Theater

Masonry hedge walls

Interior sculpture gallery

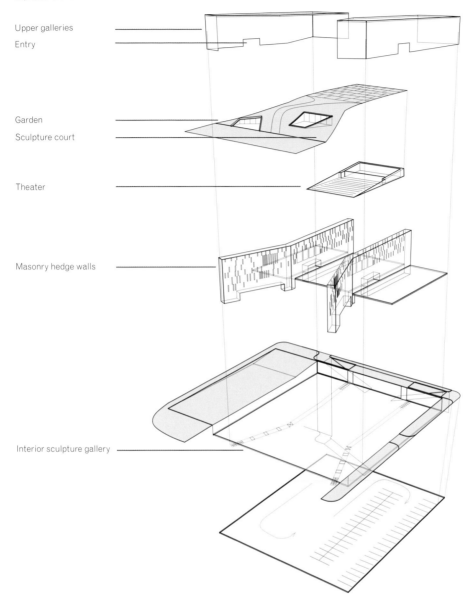

AIDS Memorial Grove, in Collaboration with Rodolphe el-Khoury

(ReK Productions)

San Francisco

Sited in San Francisco's Golden Gate Park, the proposed memorial links the intimacy of the AIDS Memorial Grove to the encompassing daily urbanism of its surrounding city. This unique memorial serves not only the solemn need to commemorate but also the need to engage our growing consciousness of AIDS as a part of life ongoing. The design of a singular landscape surface engages three major features of the Grove's expansive site: the perimeter ridge and roadway, the descending slope of the ravine, and the valley floor. The gesture redefines the roadway above the Grove, drapes the slope, and connects visitors in a sequence from street to meadow.

Projecting from the precipice wall southward, the landscape surface provides a plateau of discrete audio-reception points. An embedded constellation of sound domes enmesh natural sounds with an archive of personal stories; sound is heard clearly from a single position, fading quickly to a whisper at adjacent locations. This effect is achieved with technology that is hyperbolically zoned, with parabolas indicating a point-focused sound wave, directed for the listener to hear one stream at a time. A remote, Web-based archive transmits stories, songs, and comments from the global AIDS community to the aural field, creating a real-time memorial from which meaning is found in experience and remembered over time.

Material textures

Site plan

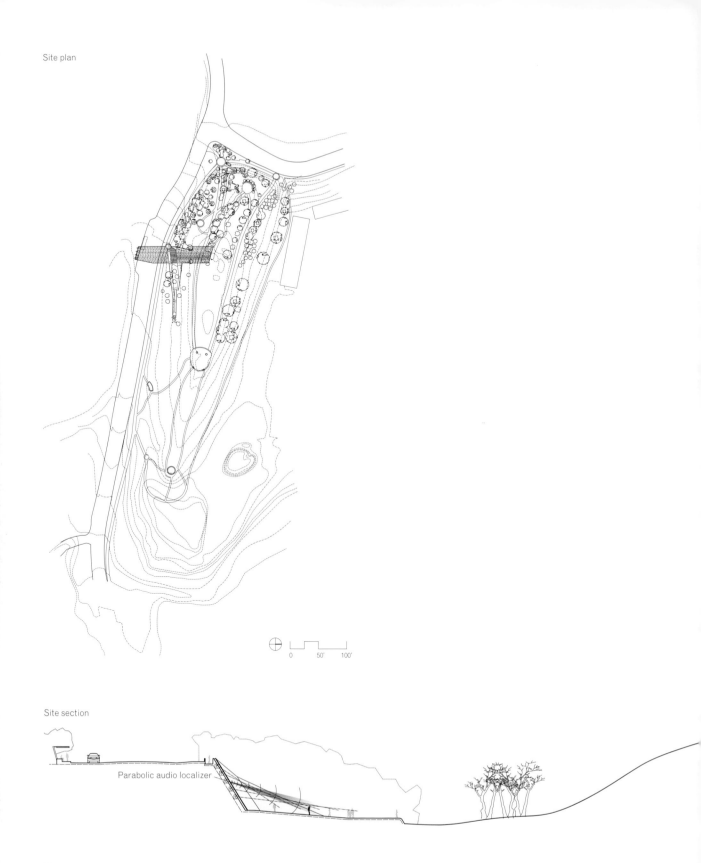

0   50'   100'

Site section

Parabolic audio localizer

Harvey Milk Memorial Car

San Francisco

This portrait of the life and work of Harvey Milk, the slain San Francisco city supervisor, brings his extraordinary call for social justice into the everyday paths of the commonplace. The environment is a streetcar set in his adopted city, but prototypically can be sited within any existing infrastructure to dynamically extend the boundaries of civic space and claim unspecified systems of connectivity. The proposal creates a "district-specific" vehicle whereby local histories, events, and communities are portrayed with integrated media of polymer light-emitting diodes (PLEDs).

The car is designed as an episodic experience, providing simultaneous information through chance encounter. An electronic digitization displays a narrative of filmic images pertaining to the life and times of the subject, while the transparent chassis exposes the shifting ground beneath. The configuration of seating transforms throughout the bays, accommodating various social settings—couples, singles, and congregate—and encouraging random and incidental groupings.

The memorial car mixes collages of commemorative images with the real-time exchange between passengers. Refracted images of data, luminous voids of surface, and reflections of surrounding urbanism are mapped across the car's exterior translucent skin. This ephemeral, mobile environment passes through the city to which Harvey Milk brought change, resisting fixed imagery and challenging the pathos of efficiency.

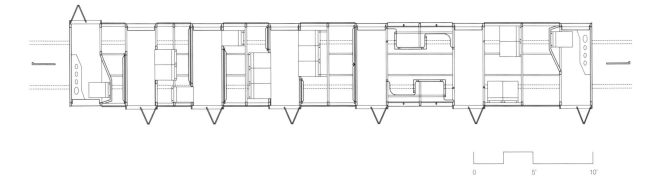

0   5'   10'

Car plan

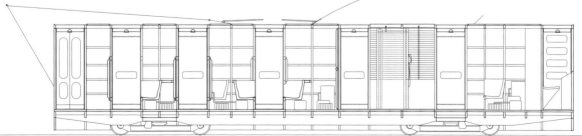

Climate Clock, in Collaboration with Bill Fontana, of Resoundings

San Jose, California

Climate Clock creates a place of physical repose and reflection that connects downtown San Jose to twelve significant ecological habitats around the world. The Clock is an instrument for listening and learning, as well as a civic space for reflection. The rotunda resonates with live sound from remote environments and displays climatic conditions within its fluid and kinetic surfaces. The experience is meant to engage the visitor in both a sensual and a cerebral connection to the global array of environments.

The Clock is composed of a dozen structurally independent carbon-fiber piers arranged in a circular pattern that torque from the ground and converge into an open oculus to frame the sky. A convex void is nested within the rotunda, forming semicircular listening and visualization niches on the interior face of the piers. Each niche will broadcast real-time audio from selected global environments and display interactive visual data on a film containing polymer light-emitting diodes (PLEDs).

Carbon-fiber fabrication is an emerging technology within the region, south of San Francisco. Each pier will be factory produced in the Bay Area, minimizing transportation and reducing site disturbances. PLED technology employed for visual display uses a fraction of the energy required by conventional display systems. Sustainable design informs all aspects of Climate Clock. Permeable surface pavers minimize water runoff, and the central water feature captures and recycles gray water. Thin-film photovoltaic cells are laminated to the outer surface of the piers, yielding sufficient power to make Climate Clock 100 percent energy-independent.

Twelve panel sections

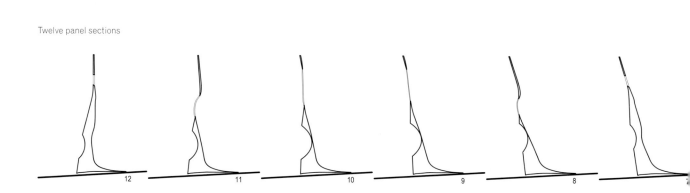

12   11   10   9   8

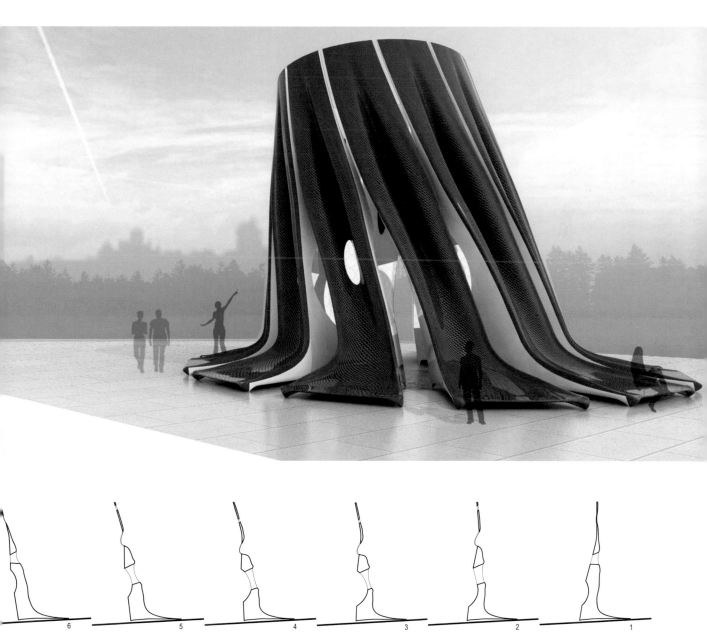

Plan

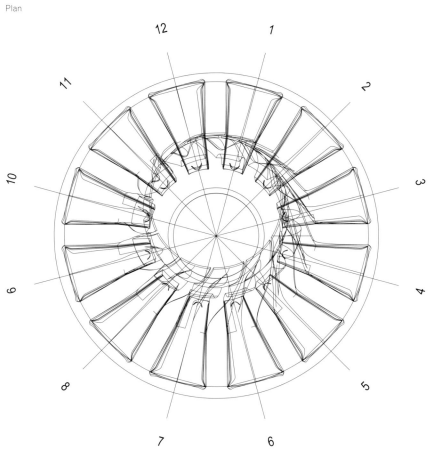

Diagrammatic section of installation sounds

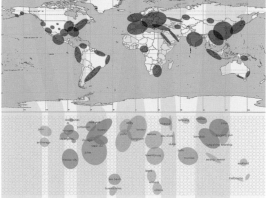

Diagram of global CO₂ display

Martyrs' Square, in Collaboration with Rodolphe el-Khoury (ReK Productions)

Beirut, Lebanon

The urban design strategy for the Martyrs' Square district focuses on the public realm, extending the urban room of the historic square to the waterfront and farther south to the elevated ring road. This new public space is defined and supported by a roof structure: an inverted landscape that both "grounds" and intensifies various activities and programs. The design is modeled on public places of old Beirut where climate-minded infrastructure—canopies, tents, and roofs—simply allow for a vibrant, sustainable inhabitation of open public space year-round.

The roofscape is a field of repetitive elements designed to perform as a shield, filter, and reflector, with emergent properties that are calibrated to suit desirable climatic conditions. The field's variable density ranges from a tight formation to a screenlike structure. Smooth, continuous inflections disperse or intensify the regularity of this roofscape to accommodate full-spectrum programs and encourage fluid scenarios of occupation and identity between uses: The Marketplace, Civic Hall, Archeological Park and Site Museum, Water-Bus/Taxi Station, Bicycle Library, Car Share, and Electric-Car Charging Stations.

The design accommodates the commonplace elements of the city while leaving the messy manifestation of urban life unchecked. Capitalizing on the infrastructural and monumental assets, the roofscape creates an extraordinary and viable public space. It serves as a catalyst for development and preserves the right for latent market forces to shape vacant adjacent lots.

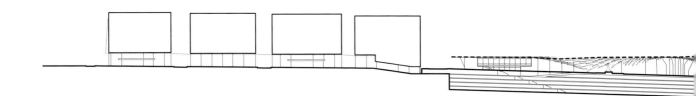

Site section

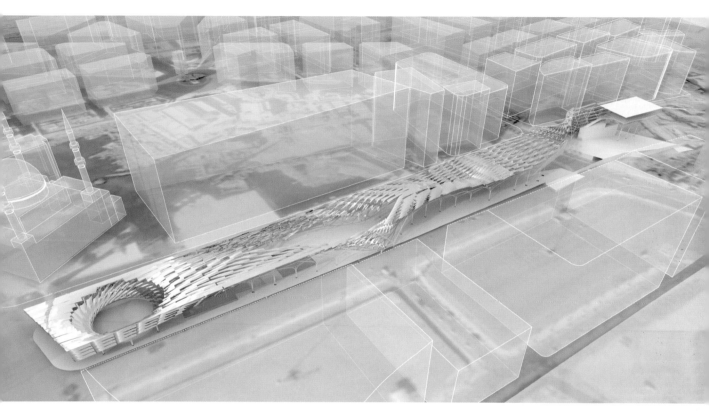

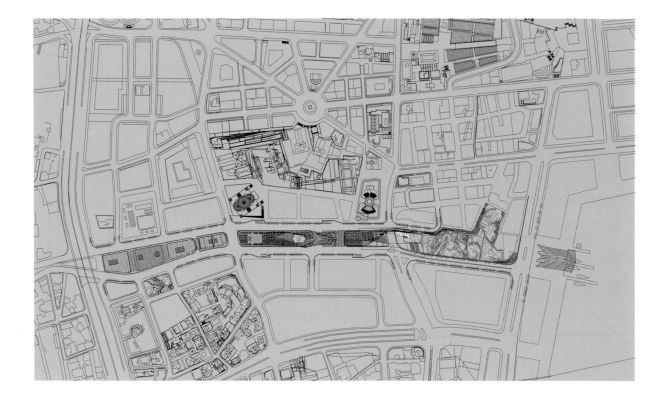

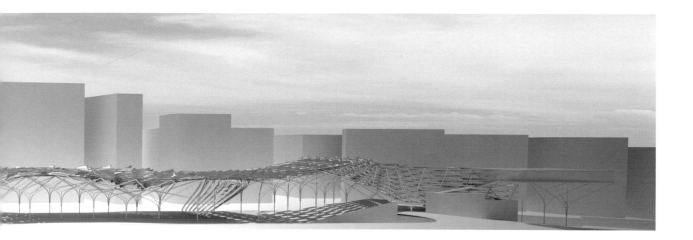

SKIN/fabric: The locally aggregated patchwork, emblematic of shade structures intrinsic to the region, is reinterpreted as a repetitive pixilated field/fabric—a continuously modulated skin that is differentially aggregated and deformed in response to material forces acting on the site. Local processes of additive accumulation, the markers of material occupation, are transformed by the continuity of the whole, just as the bifurcating double-sided membrane is split between the discrete grounded elements that

it collects and the floating ephemera that are fluidly dispersed across its surface. Like the surface of paradox, which always pulls in two directions at once, this feathered skin acts as a medium to both absorb and reveal difference, furnishing continuity while enabling the registration of local intensities—material indexes—that are embedded within the very medium from which they emerge.

–I. B.

Mission Bay: A Proposal for a Green District Identity

Green Belt, Eco-Magnet High School, and CCA's Student and Media Center

San Francisco

San Francisco is known for its character and strong neighborhood identity. Its districts are defined by unique urban typologies where the city grid intersects with the beauty of its exaggerated geography. The newest district is Mission Bay, a flat, 303-acre parcel with 41 acres of open space, bracketed by the San Francisco Bay and Interstate 280. It is home to the San Francisco Giants, the Research Campus of the University of California–San Francisco, and emerging biotech and media industries, along with some six thousand units of new housing and six million square feet of commercial and new municipal facilities.

The Master Plan Proposal features an Eco-Park with gardens and facilities that reinstate the district's lost ecology and habitats. Also included are proposals for California College of the Arts' San Francisco campus and a new Eco-Magnet High School for Environmental Studies, along with municipal facilities. The Eco-Park and the high school are interdependent with the natural ecology and cultural community of the district. The high school is designed as a high-performance building, though, more important, it offers a key integer in the sustainable operation of the community. The proposal for CCA's Student and Media Center provides a cultural anchor to the district.

The Green District Identity Plan puts forth a new, sustainable agenda for Mission Bay. A Green Enterprise Zone of businesses dedicated to energy and material mindfulness defines Mission Bay as a central destination for surrounding neighborhoods, thus enhancing identity, thresholds, streetscape, and green space.

Activating the district's margins at key points along the Mission Creek canal, with a new pedestrian bridge at 5th Street—and enhancing the threshold at Interstate 280 with a skateboard park and an art-lighting project—will strengthen key connections back to the city and will also open the district to adjacent neighborhoods.

FRAGMENT/field: Revitalizing the urban is enabled by reinserting "wild" nature back into the marginal and eroded spaces of our cultural habitat. Abandoned urban fragments are reconnected through the overlay of continuous ecologies—networks of intensely programmed spaces that become material markers of an evolving acculturated nature. These domesticated ecological insertions, whose multiplicity is characteristic of both fields and flocks, operate as a matrix of discrete urban details intended to collectively transform and regenerate the urban environment in which they are situated.
–I. B.

Solar Farm
Four million square feet
of dedicated rooftop
for photovoltaic energy
production

Wastewater
Districtwide water collection
system and on-site
wastewater treatment

High-Performance
Buildings
Districtwide requirement
of LEED-certified high-
performance buildings

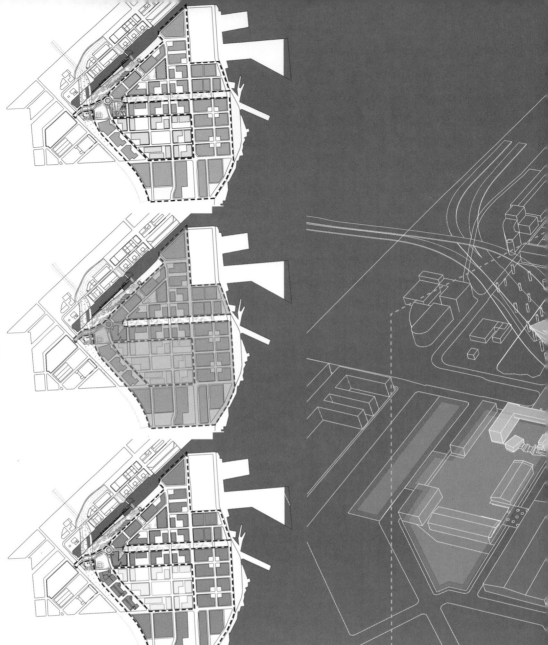

Pedestrian Street Bridge

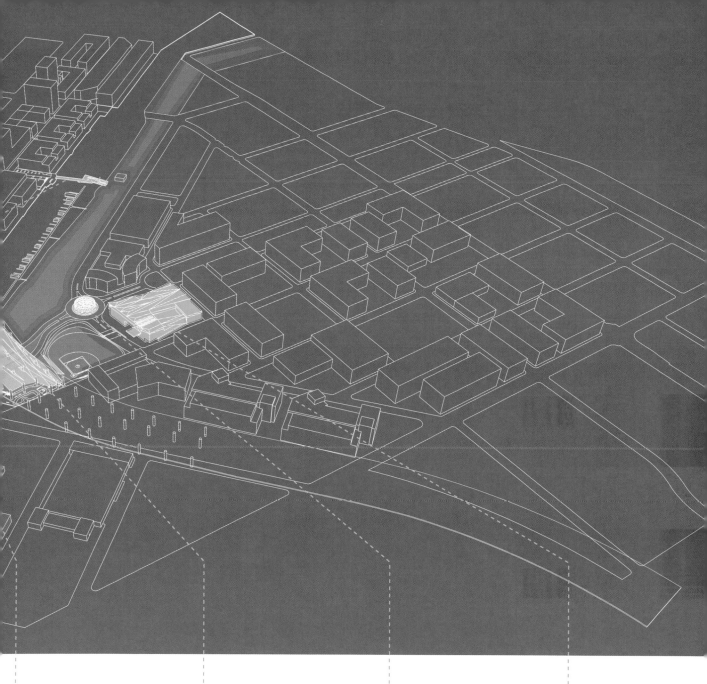

CCA Commons

Skateboard Park

Aviary

Eco-Magnet High School

Green Enterprise Zone diagrams and site interventions

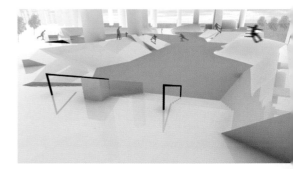

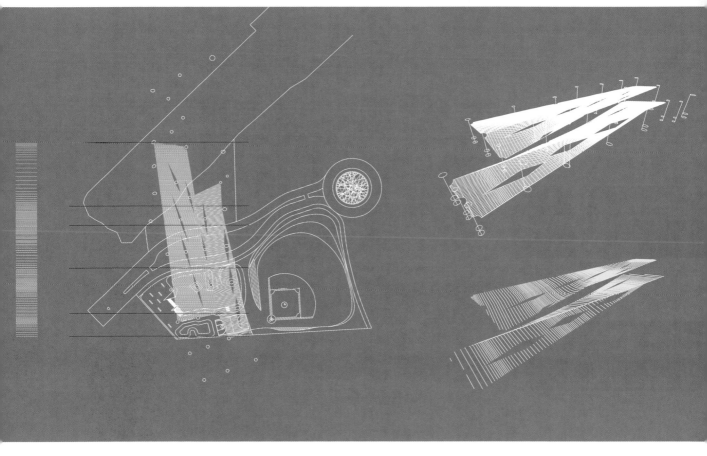

SKATEBOARD PARK AND LIGHTWAY / FREEWAY INSTALLATION

A skateboard park and an art-lighting project transform an enhanced gateway at Interstate 280. These will promote a habitable civic space for pedestrians, skateboarders, and bicyclists by day, while illuminating the freeway overpass for a safe, vibrant nightscape.

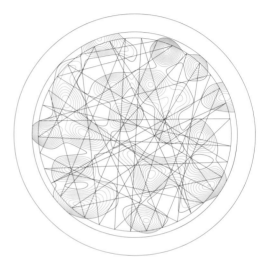

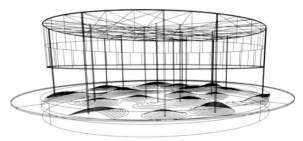

PEDESTRIAN STREET BRIDGE AND AVIARY

The pedestrian bridge over 5th Street serves a double function as a civic space, reconnecting San Francisco's downtown to its South of Market district, and expanding the existing Mission Creek Park to the water's edge. The proposed aviary, west of the bridge, is sited on a traffic circle; it provides a new green-marker for the migratory path of birds.

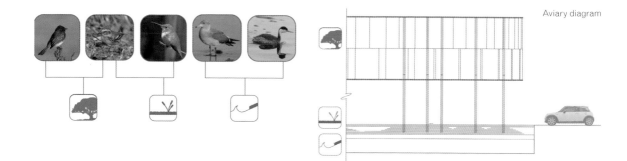

Aviary diagram

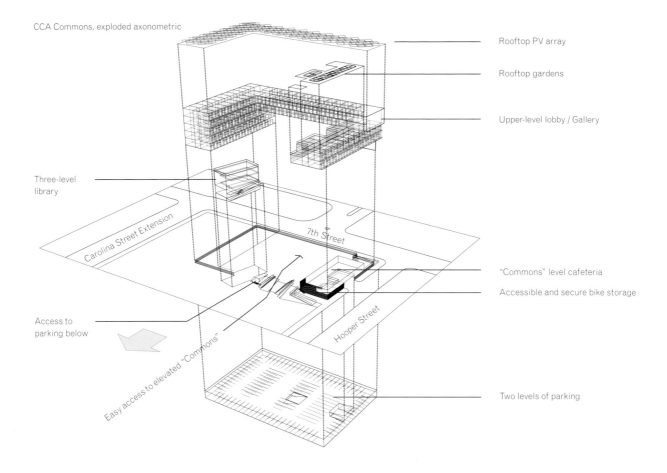

CCA Commons, exploded axonometric

Rooftop PV array

Rooftop gardens

Upper-level lobby / Gallery

Three-level library

Carolina Street Extension

7th Street

"Commons" level cafeteria

Accessible and secure bike storage

Access to parking below

Hooper Street

Easy access to elevated "Commons"

Two levels of parking

A PROPOSAL FOR CCA COMMONS

San Francisco's design district is anchored by the California College of the Arts campus, which is home to the college's graduate programs and undergraduate programs in architecture and design, as well as to the Wattis Institute for Contemporary Art. The CCA Commons houses the Student and Media Center, extending the campus to the periphery of Interstate 280 immediately west of the Mission Bay District. The private institutional building expands its programming to serve the greater design community with a gallery, a cafe, a black-box theater, and an outdoor amphitheater. The CCA Commons is a didactic project, designed as a zero-carbon, high-performance building that integrates on-site renewable energy systems, uses responsible waste-management and water-conservation practices, and is programmed to encourage clean-air transit.

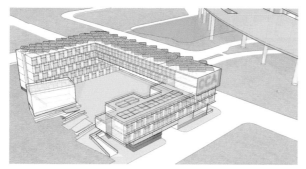

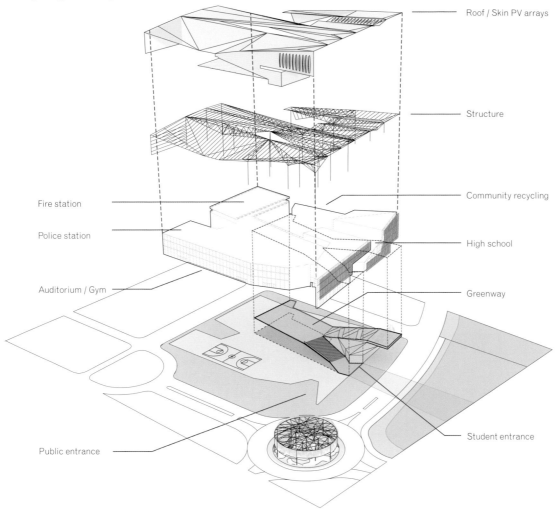

Eco-Magnet High School, exploded axonometric

Roof / Skin PV arrays

Structure

Community recycling

Fire station

Police station

High school

Auditorium / Gym

Greenway

Public entrance

Student entrance

A PROPOSAL FOR ECO-MAGNET HIGH SCHOOL AND MUNICIPAL BUILDING

Designed as a large, multipurpose facility, a proposed Eco-Magnet High School and Municipal Building contains a high school, police and fire stations, and a community recycling center, all sharing structural, environmental, and waste systems. The school is organized around an open courtyard—a greenway that connects the entry to the ascending roof gardens. The building opens dramatically to the public, offering a communal gathering space in the auditorium/gym, as well as a gallery for use by both students and the public. The project is designed as a model of how buildings can serve, in a deep way, the environment and its community, demonstrating the potential for interconnectedness between urbanism and natural ecologies.

Folding Water: A Ventilated Levee for a Living Estuary

San Francisco Estuary and Delta, California

Folding Water is a ventilated levee that protects shorelines by regulating both rising sea levels and the delta and bay waters. Responding to dramatic global and climatic transformations, this dynamic levee system preserves waterfront property, maintains areas for recreation and tourism, and conserves the estuarine ecosystem that is dependent on tidal action. It departs from the conventional, static levee—or dam—by exchanging waters through a perforated pump wall to artificially manage tides and to create microbay estuaries along the shoreline of San Francisco and other key areas within the bay. These estuarine re-creations, or Bay Avatars, mirror the shoreline's current water levels, activity, and ecology, sustaining the relationship between the estuary and its inhabitants. The subaquatic structure of the proposed levee integrates geothermal energy plants, tidal turbines to harvest wave energy, desalination facilities, and wastewater disposal. This megascaled civic project provides a vital portal for the cultural and environmental future of the region in the form of a monumental "fold" of water.

The proposal for Folding Water centers on an idea of infrastructure that registers experience in real time to internalize the values of ecological and cultural sustainability. This proposal reallocates the understanding of infrastructure from a massive, dissociative intervention to a phenomenological experience that conflates the variable nature of perception and the ever-changing conditions of the environment. Folding Water, though expansive and monumental in scale, provides visual and corporeal interactions within partial and intimate moments.

Hardshore protection:
Levees along developed
shorelines and farmlands

Shoreline protection:
Tidal marshes + wetlands

Ocean
Folding water
Bay water

FOLD/wave: The fold is a detail drawn from the logic of matter—an index of fluid forces revealed in the tidal patterns of the oceanic surface and the intricate undulations of coastal topographies. In the proposed seawall, where monumentality is produced by stretching the discrete architectural object to the scale of the geographic, the fold is strategically architecturalized through its planimetric and sectional elaboration. This tactical enfolding of nature-with-artifice employs the continuity of the fold to simultaneously capture, regulate, and recircuit the movements of water and energy, bodies and infrastructural networks. The seawall's attenuated boundary will furnish an expanded surface for exchange, to increase the potential productive "resourcing" of untapped dynamic forces.

–I. B.

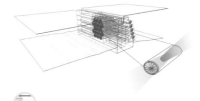

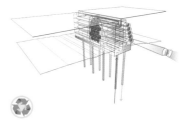

Water Level Management: The Fold

Tidal Management: The Ventilator

Self-Sustaining Energy: Geothermal and Tidal

Project Index Timeline

1   2   3   4

1991

3X3 + 9, THE ARCHITECTURAL FOUNDATION AND 2AES, THE CONTRACT DESIGN CENTER, SF
EXHIBITION

1992

ARCHITECTURE REPRESENTED/FURNITURE REALIZED, CLOCKTOWER, SF
EXHIBITION

1

HORIZON HOUSE: SFMOMA PERMANENT COLLECTION
PROPOSAL

1993

BEST OF CATEGORY FOR ENVIRONMENTS, *I.D. MAGAZINE*
AWARD

CITY ROOM GARDEN: COLLEGES OF ARCHITECTURE AT TEXAS A&M AND UNIVERSIITY OF HOUSTON, TEXAS A&M, UNIVERSIITY OF HOUSTON, CALIFORNIA COLLEGE OF ARTS AND CRAFTS
EXHIBITION

1994

PRIVATE RESIDENCE AND LEF FOUNDATION OFFICES / GALLERY
PROJECT

AIA NATIONAL HONOR AWARD: INTERIORS, AIA, NATIONAL COUNCIL
AWARD

AIA STATE HONOR AWARD: RENOVATION, AIA, CALIFORNIA STATE COUNCIL
AWARD

AIA REGIONAL HONOR AWARD, INTERIORS, AIA, SAN FRANCISCO CHAPTER
AWARD

YOUNG ARCHITECTS, THE ARCHITECTURAL LEAGUE OF NEW YORK, 13TH ANNUAL YOUNG ARCHITECTS FORUM
AWARD

YOUNG ARCHITECTS FORUM, ARCHITECTURAL LEAGUE OF NEW YORK
EXHIBITION

NEW COUNTY: RURAL HOMES IN CALIFORNIA'S WINE REGION, LIMN GALLERY, SF
EXHIBITION

2

E-BOX: SFMOMA PERMANENT COLLECTION
INTSALLATION

FETISH: SFMOMA PERMANENT COLLECTION
INTSALLATION

1995

FIRST PLACE: RESIDENTIAL DESIGN COMPETITION, *LANDSCAPE ARCHITECTURE MAGAZINE*
AWARD

"SEX SELLS": UC BERKELEY MUSEUM AND PACIFIC FILM ARCHIVE, RENA BRANSTON GALLERY
EXHIBITION

ADDISON

1998

MILL VALLEY RESIDENCE
PROJECT

FABRICATIONS: SFMOMA AND THE WEXNER CENTER FOR THE ARTS
EXHIBITION

1999

FRANCES

BODY IN REPOSE
INTSALLATION

I.D. MAGAZINE, BEST OF CATEGORY FOR ENVIRONMENTS
AWARD

3

SFAI AUDITORIUM & STUDENT SERVICES
PROJECT

MARTIN LUTHER KING, JR. MEMORIAL
PROPOSAL

DESIGN VANGUARD AWARD, *ARCHITECTURAL RECORD MAGAZINE*
AWARD

200

SCHOOL OF DESIGN, CAMBRIDGE, MA
EXHIBITION

"2X2: ARCHITECTURAL COLLABORATIONS," UC
BERKELEY ART MUSEUM AND PACIFIC FILM ARCHIVE
EXHIBITION

JEWISH COMMUNITY CENTER PRESCHOOL
PROJECT

NOB HILL RESIDENCE
PROJECT

2001

HARVEY MILK MEMORIAL TRANSIT
PROPOSAL

DESIGN DISTINCTION--ENVIRONMENTS
CATEGORY, *I.D. MAGAZINE* ANNUAL DESIGN
REVIEW, 47TH ANNUAL AWARDS
AWARD

AIA STATE HONOR AWARD: EXCELLENCE
IN SINGLE-FAMILY RESIDENTIAL DESIGN,
AIA, CALIFORNIA STATE COUNCIL
AWARD

GRACE

MILLENNIUM ISSUE EXHIBITION FOR *ARCHITECTURAL
RECORD*, GAMMEL DOK - THE DANISH ARCHITECTURAL
ASSOC OFFICIAL EXHIBITION SPACE, COPENHAGEN
EXHIBITION

DUMBOX, PA, INTERACTIVE MEDIA
KIOSK AT 43 MERCER STREET, NYC
EXHIBITION

LODI BUNKHOUSE
PROJECT

2002

LICK-WILMERDING HIGH SCHOOL
PROPOSAL

EMERGING VOICES, ARCHITECTURAL
LEAGUE OF NEW YORK, YOUNG
ARCHITECT'S FORUM
AWARD

WHEREABOUTS: NEW ARCHITEC-
TURES WITH LOCAL IDENTITIES,
CITY UNIVERSITY OF NEW YORK
EXHIBITION

725 GREENWICH TENANT IMPROVEMENT
PROJECT

PARK PRESIDIO RESIDENCE
PROJECT

RISD STUDENT CENTER
PROPOSAL

INTERLOCHEN ARTS ACADEMY
PROPOSAL

SONOMA COUNTY ARTS MUSEUM
PROPOSAL

2003

PENTAGON MEMORIAL
PROPOSAL

EXCELLENCE IN UNBUILT DESIGN,
AIA BEST OF THE BAY
AWARD

SF MOMA: THE ART OF DESIGN: WORKS OF
ARCHITECTURE, GRAPHIC DESIGN & INDUSTRIAL
DESIGN FROM THE PERMANENT COLLECTION
EXHIBITION

CALISTOGA RESIDENCE
PROJECT

SJSU MUSEUM OF ART & DESIGN
RESEARCH

4

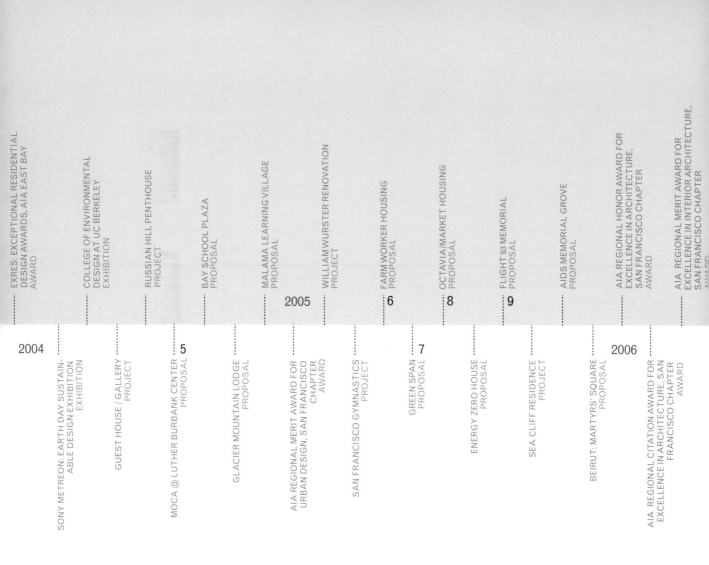

8

9

EXRES: EXCEPTIONAL RESIDENTIAL
DESIGN AWARDS, AIA EAST BAY
AWARD

COLLEGE OF ENVIRONMENTAL
DESIGN AT UC BERKELEY
EXHIBITION

RUSSIAN HILL PENTHOUSE
PROJECT

BAY SCHOOL PLAZA
PROPOSAL

MALAMA LEARNING VILLAGE
PROPOSAL

2005

WILLIAM WURSTER RENOVATION
PROJECT

FARM WORKER HOUSING
PROPOSAL

6

OCTAVIA/MARKET HOUSING
PROPOSAL

8

FLIGHT 93 MEMORIAL
PROPOSAL

9

AIDS MEMORIAL GROVE
PROPOSAL

AIA REGIONAL HONOR AWARD FOR
EXCELLENCE IN ARCHITECTURE,
SAN FRANCISCO CHAPTER
AWARD

AIA REGIONAL MERIT AWARD FOR
EXCELLENCE IN INTERIOR ARCHITECTURE,
SAN FRANCISCO CHAPTER

2004

SONY METREON: EARTH DAY SUSTAIN-
ABLE DESIGN EXHIBITION
EXHIBITION

GUEST HOUSE / GALLERY
PROJECT

MOCA @ LUTHER BURBANK CENTER
PROPOSAL

5

GLACIER MOUNTAIN LODGE
PROPOSAL

AIA REGIONAL MERIT AWARD FOR
URBAN DESIGN, SAN FRANCISCO
CHAPTER
AWARD

SAN FRANCISCO GYMNASTICS
PROJECT

GREEN SPAN
PROPOSAL

7

ENERGY ZERO HOUSE
PROPOSAL

SEA CLIFF RESIDENCE
PROJECT

BEIRUT: MARTYRS' SQUARE
PROPOSAL

2006

AIA REGIONAL CITATION AWARD FOR
EXCELLENCE IN ARCHITECTURE, SAN
FRANCISCO CHAPTER
AWARD

SERENITY DENTAL SPA
PROJECT

AIA REGIONAL HONOR AWARD FOR UNBUILT DESIGN, SAN FRANCISCO CHAPTER
AWARD

PATTERSON DENTAL SUITE
PROJECT

MISSION BAY
PROPOSAL

2008

RUBIN RESIDENCE
PROJECT

PALO ALTO RESIDENCE
PROJECT

SAN FRANCISCO GREEN DENTAL LEED SILVER CERTIFICATION
AWARD

MASS 495 MIXED USE DEVELOPMENT
PROPOSAL

12

LA LINER
PROPOSAL

13

CONTEMPORARY ART MUSEUM AT THE PRESIDIO
PROPOSAL

TIBURON RESIDENCE & POOLHOUSE
UNDER CONSTRUCTION

THETOOTHSPA
UNDER CONSTRUCTION

WINNER, RISING TIDES: AN INTERNATIONAL IDEAS COMPETITION FOR RISING SEA LEVELS
AWARD

10

11

PROJECT

SFMOMA SCULPTURE GARDEN
PROPOSAL

NEUTRON
FEASIBILITY

2007

JAY'S DELI
PROJECT

"FOLDING WATER: CITY OF THE FUTURE," FERRY BUILDING, SAN FRANCISCO
EXHIBITION

HILLSBOROUGH RESIDENCE
PROJECT

MOUNTAIN VIEW FAMILY DENTISTRY
PROJECT

CLIMATE CLOCK
PROPOSAL

GROUND UP SYRACUSE
PROPOSAL

FOLDING WATER: CITY OF THE FUTURE
PROPOSAL

SAN RAFAEL RESIDENCE
UNDER CONSTRUCTION

PENINSULA ENDODONTICS GROUP
UNDER CONSTRUCTION

RANIERI RESIDENCE, MASSACHUSETTS
PROJECT

FINALIST, CITY OF PHOENIX GIMME SHELTER COMPETITION
AWARD

Awards

1993
Best of Category for Environments, *I.D. Magazine*
AIA National Honor Award: Interiors, AIA, National
 Council
AIA State Honor Award: Renovation, AIA, California State
 Council
AIA Regional Honor Award: Interiors, AIA, San Francisco
 Chapter
Young Architects, Architectural League of New York, 13th
 Annual Young Architects Forum

1995
First Place: Residential Design Competition, *Landscape
 Architecture Magazine*

1999
Best of Category for Environments, *I.D. Magazine*, for
 Fabrications: Body in Repose

2000
Design Vanguard Award, *Architectural Record Magazine*

2001
Design Distinction—Environments Category, *I.D. Magazine*
 Annual Design Review, 47th Annual Awards, for Nob
 Hill Residence
Honor Award: Excellence in Single-Family Residential
 Design, AIA, California State Council, for Nob Hill
 Residence

2002
Emerging Voices, Architectural League of New York,
 Young Architects Forum

2003
Excellence in Unbuilt Design, AIA Best of the Bay, for
 Harvey Milk Memorial Car
ExRes: Exceptional Residential Design Awards, AIA East
 Bay, for Lodi Bunkhouse

2004
AIA San Francisco Best of the Bay: Merit Award for Urban
 Design, for Beirut: Martyrs' Square

2005
AIA San Francisco Best of the Bay Award: Excellence in
 Architecture Honor Award

2006
AIA San Francisco Best of the Bay: Excellence in
 Architecture Citation Award, for Guesthouse / Gallery
AIA San Francisco Best of the Bay: Excellence in Interior
 Architecture Merit Award, for William Wurster
 Renovation
AIA San Francisco Best of the Bay: Honor Award, for Lodi
 Bunkhouse and LEF Foundation / Napa Residence

2007
AIA San Francisco Best of the Bay: Excellence in Unbuilt
 Design Honor Award, for Eco-Magnet High School
 and Municipal Building

2009
Winner, Rising Tides: International Ideas Competition for
 Rising Sea Levels, sponsored by The San Francisco
 Bay Conservation and Development Commission, for
 Folding Water
Finalist, Gimme Shelter Competition, sponsored by
 The City of Phoenix, Arizona, Public Art Program,
 for Linking Shade

Selected Bibliography

Another 100 of the World's Best Houses. Victoria, Australia: Images Publishing Group, 2003.

Bishop, Deborah. "Spacing Out." *Dwell Magazine*, May 2006.

Betsky, Aaron. "A Row House by Kuth/Ranieri Presents a Mysterious Facade to a San Francisco Street." *Architecture Magazine*, August 2000.

———. "Industrial Chic." *Metropolitan Home*, September 1996.

———. "Urban Living in a Country Barn." *Los Angeles Times Magazine*, September 1996.

Caille, Emmanuel. "Les Grands Meubles." *AMC Le Moniteur Architecture*, December 2001.

Carter, Brian, and Annette Lecuyer. *All American: Innovation in American Architecture.* New York: Thames & Hudson Ltd., 2002.

"Design Distinction—Environments Category" for the *Guesthouse / Gallery. I.D. Magazine,* I.D. Annual Design Review.

"Environments, Best of Category Award." *I.D. Magazine*, Annual Design Review, July/August 1993.

"Environments, Design Distinction Award." *I.D. Magazine*, Annual Design Review, August 2001.

Futagawa, Yoshio, ed. *GA Houses* 67, August 2001.

Gorlin, Alexander. *Creating the New American Townhouse.* New York: Rizzoli International Publications, 2005.

International Architecture Yearbook. Vol. 8. Victoria, Australia: Images Publishing Group, 2002.

Jacobson, Karen, ed. *Fabrications.* San Francisco: San Francisco Museum of Modern Art, 1998. Essays by Aaron Betsky, Pat Morton, Mark Robbins, and Terence Tiley.

Kliczkowski, Guillermo Raul. *32 Viviendas En Estados Unidos II.* Madrid: Casa International, 1994.

Kuth/Ranieri. "The Body in Repose, An Installation for 'Fabrications' at SFMOMA." *On-Site Magazine*, Fall 2003.

Ngo, Dung, and Adi Shamir Zion. *Open House: Unbound Space and the Modern Dwelling.* New York: Rizzoli International Publications. 2002.

"The 1995 AIA Honor Awards." *Architecture Magazine*, May 1995.

Ojeda, Oscar. *The New American House.* New York: Whitney Library of Design, 1995.

Olmstead, Marty. "Up Stairs Down." *Appellation*, April/May 1996.

1,000 Architects. Victoria, Australia: Images Publishing Group, 2003.

"Opening the Garden: Residential Design Competition." *Landscape Architecture*, April 1995.

Rope, Kate. "Tomorrowland: Meet the Bay Area Futurists." *San Francisco Magazine*, January 2000.

Rosa, Joe. "Future." *Surface Magazine*, S.F. Bay Area Architecture Supplement, September 2003.

Saeks, Diane Dorran. "Modern Lightness." *San Francisco Magazine*, November 2007.

San Francisco Design Awards. *California Home & Design.* May 2007: 132–43.

"San Francisco Modern." *Modern Living*, September 1995.

Sardar, Zahid. "All Things Great and Small." *San Francisco Examiner Magazine*, September 17, 2000.

———. "Solar Supporter." *San Francisco Chronicle Magazine*, September 7, 2003.

Schwarzer, Mitchell. *Architecture of the San Francisco Bay Area: A History + Guide.* San Francisco: William Stout, 2006.

Silander, Lisa. "Hot Houses, Cool Designs." *RISD Views*, Summer 2001.

Sirefman, Susanna. *Whereabouts: New Architectures with Local Identities.* New York: Monacelli Press, 2003.

Sweeney, Sidney. "Industrial Living." *Design for Living Magazine*, Spring 2005.

Sweet, Fay, ed. *Interior Details.* London: Mitchell Beazley, 2002.

Temko, Sussanah. "Looking Below the Surface." *Competitions*, Fall 2001.

Tierney, Therese. "AIACC 2001 DESIGN AWARDS, Iann Stolz Residence." *arcCA*, September 2001.

Trulove, James Grayson, and Il Kim, ed. *The New American House Additions and Renovations*. New York: Whitney Library of Design, 2001.

———. *The New American House.* New York: Whitney Library of Design, 2003.

Urbach, Henry. "Building for Now: Three Museums Try to Make Architecture 'Immediate' for All of Us." *Metropolis*, May 1998.

Urban Houses. Barcelona: Links International Publications, 2002.

Vivanco, Sandra. "Private Residence and Office Gallery for the LEF Foundation." *Domus Internationale*, May 1995.

Weathersby Jr., William. "Kuth/Ranieri Explores the Applications and Ambiguities of Industrial Materials." *Architectural Record*, December 2000.

Webb, Michael. "Greene House." *Interiors Magazine*, November 1996.

Weingarten, David. *Bay Area Style: San Francisco Bay Region Houses 1893–2004.* New York: Rizzoli International Publications, 2003.

"The Young Architects Forum 1994." *L'arca* 82, May 1994.

Contributors

Ila Berman
Director of Architecture
California College of the Arts, San Francisco

Aaron Betsky
Director, Cincinnati Art Museum

Rudolphe el-Khoury
Canada Research Chair in Architecture and Urban Design
Associate Professor, University of Toronto, John H. Daniels
School of Architecture, Landscape, and Design
Partner, Khoury Levit Fong

Mitchell Schwarzer
Professor, Visual Studies
California College of the Arts, San Francisco

Landscape Architects:

Andrea Cochran
Andrea Cochran Landscape Architecture
Guesthouse / Gallery
Hillsborough Residence
William Wurster Renovation

Ron Lutsko Jr.
Lutsko Associates Landscape Architects
LEF / Private Residence

Gary Strang
GLS Landscape Architecture
Park Presidio Residence

Consultant:

Mark Stacy
Professor, Civil and Environmental Engineering
University of California, Berkeley
Folding Water: A Ventilated Levee for a Living Estuary

Profiles

Byron Kuth FAIA, LEED AP and Elizabeth Ranieri AIA, LEED AP began their partnership after earning degrees in architecture and fine arts from the Rhode Island School of Design. Upon relocating to San Francisco from Boston, they established Kuth/Ranieri Architects in 1990. Both have taught at California College of the Arts, Harvard University's Graduate School of Design, and as Freidman Professors at the University of California, Berkeley. Over the course of two decades they have practiced in a studio environment where concepts are explored collaboratively with their team of architects and designers. Steve Const, LEED AP joined their practice in 1994 while earning a degree in architecture from the California College of the Arts. In 2005 he became an Associate Partner and manages Kuth/Ranieri's Sustainable Commercial Interiors Practice Group.

 Kuth/Ranieri Architects participated in the multimedia group show "Fabrications" exhibited at SFMOMA, MOMA, and the Wexner Center, and has won several national, state, and regional AIA awards, the Architectural League's "Young Architects" and "Emerging Voices" awards, and *I.D. Magazine's* 39th, 45th, and 47th Annual Awards. Exhibits include the UC Berkeley Sustainable Design Exhibition, 2004; and "City of the Future," an Invited Competition and Exhibit, sponsored by the History Channel, 2008.

 To promote and improve education and understanding of architecture and urbanism for a broad cross section of civic audiences, Kuth/Ranieri established Deep Green Design Alliance (DGDA) in 2006, a think tank to further the study of sustainable industries and community empowerment.

Studio Members

Erik Bloom
Michael Brehmer
Justin Cipriani
Joelle Colliard
Steve Const
David Dayan
Andrew Dunbar
Jee Hee Haar Farris
Michelle Fornabai
David Gill
Ross Hummel
Matt Hutchinson
Chelsea Johnson
Ryan Kennihan
Jonathan Kuzmich
Maynard Leon
Elmer Lin
Lauren MacColl
Andre Mandel
Sarah Manning
Peter Mavridis

Dave Maynard
Claudia Merzario
Brian Milman
Balz Mueller
Nathan Nagai
Naoko Ono
Jeffrey Prose
Sean Pulsifer
Dave Robb
Tim Rouch
Rebecca Sharkey
Charlie Stott
Les Taylor
Mikhelle Taylor
Douglas Thornley
Sean Tracy
Gretta Tritch
Heather Walls
Kale Wisnia
Jungmi Won